Great Moments
in
Catholic History

Nihil Obstat:

> Arthur J. Scanlan, S.T.D.,
> *Censor Librorum.*

Imprimatur:

> ✠Patrick Cardinal Hayes,
> *Archbishop of New York.*

New York, May 25 1938

GREAT MOMENTS
in
CATHOLIC HISTORY

{ 100 MEMORABLE EVENTS IN CATHOLIC
HISTORY TOLD IN PICTURE AND STORY }

by

REV. EDWARD LODGE CURRAN, Ph.D.

Illustrated by

SAMUEL NISENSON

Cover image: *The Conversion on the Way to Damascus* by Caravaggio
Web Gallery of Art: Image, Public Domain, https://commons.wikimedia.org/w/index.php?curid=363483

Cover and interior book design by Mary Jo Loboda

ISBN: 978-0-9976647-7-5

Hillside Education
475 Bidwell Hill Road
Lake Ariel, PA 18436
www.hillsideeducation.com

Contents

Foreword

HOW many Catholics know the great outstanding events in the history of the Catholic Church? Sometime, as a mere social diversion, give your friends or relatives or visitors a sheet of paper and a pencil. Ask them to write down the subjects or titles which they think should be included in the present volume.

The results of such a friendly test will be amazing. How little, after all, we Catholics know about the beginning, the struggles, the accomplishments and the recent history of the Church!

What do we know about the Middle Ages? What was the Edict of Milan? What change did it bring about in the life of the early Church? Why is it correct to call the Catholic Church the first great union organizer in the world?

The answer to these and thousands of other questions will be found within the covers of this book. The history of the Church has been full of color and action. This is indicated by the beautiful drawings which precede the text.

The history of the Church must be made known to Catholic youth today. This is the most important task of the older Catholic generation. Therefore the description of one hundred outstanding events in the life of the Church appears in clear and simple language.

The writer has also endeavored to present the events in such a way that his presentation of them will be welcomed by elementary school students and university graduates alike.

The present volume answers a real need in the Catholic life of our times. There are many splendid volumes on the history of the Catholic Church. The Church has produced many of the world's finest and most brilliant historians. Their works fill shelf after shelf of Catholic college and university libraries. Some of their works may be procured from the shelves of our public libraries.

However, the Catholic who must lead an active life has no time to turn the pages of these masterpieces. Their scientific character, indicated by page after page of bibliography and footnotes, repels rather than attracts the every day reader. They are written for the advanced student rather than for the ordinary citizen of the Mystical Body of Christ.

Nor are the customary textbooks of Catholic history, found in the desks of our Catholic students at school, exactly fitted to meet the needs of the Catholic man and woman who wish to know something about the history of their Church. Such textbooks are planned for classroom discussion and not for general reading. As a result, even the textbook reading of Catholic history too often ceases with graduation from Catholic schools.

It has been the aim of the publishers and the artist and the writer to meet all these complex needs in one volume. The present volume should be part of the supplementary reading in the seventh and eighth grades of every Catholic elementary school. It should likewise find a place in every Catholic home throughout the United States. No study club can afford to be without it. High school and college students will find its summary treatment of one hundred outstanding events most helpful and most refreshing. Each narrated event can be used as the theme of a talk on the Catholic platform or of a sermon in the Catholic pulpit.

The Catholic who reads this volume will have the correct Catholic background for an understanding of current world events. He will know the truth, and the truth, as Our Lord and Savior Jesus Christ has promised, will make him free. He will be free from the ignorance and prejudices of those minds that know not the history of the Church or whose knowledge of the Church is gathered from prejudiced and unfriendly sources. The publishers of this volume have performed a task which merits the gratitude of every Catholic in the United States of America.

There is no more loyal congregation in the world than the membership of the Holy Roman Catholic Church. Catholic loyalty should be given not merely to the Church as she exists today but to the Church throughout every century of her long existence.

Catholics know that their Church was founded by Christ who is God. The foundation of the Church by Christ, who is God, is an historical fact. Catholics know that it is to their Church that the world owes both its Christianity and its civilization. A knowledge of the facts contained in this volume will justify the loyalty which they have always given to the Church of which they are a part.

In a sense not appreciated by the outside world every Catholic is the Catholic Church. All Catholics together constitute the Mystical Body of Christ and every Catholic is a necessary part of that Mystical Body.

There is no distinction of membership in the Catholic Church. The little child approaching the Communion Rail for the first time is as much a member of the Catholic Church as the Pope in Vatican City, or the Bishop of the diocese. That is what Our Lord meant to convey when He said: "I am the vine; ye are the branches."

He made no distinction between the branches at the top and the branches at the bottom; between the long branches and the short branches; between the branches that give much shade and the branches that are naked in the noonday sun; between the branches that are laden with fruit and the branches that are merely kissed with blossoms.

Christ is the vine and all of us—Pope, Cardinal, Archbishop, Bishop, Monsignor, Pastor, Curate, Nuns, Brothers, Men, Women and Children—are the branches. The only branches that fall from the vine are those who repudiate the Church or who cut themselves off through the commission of mortal sin. And even they may be grafted once again upon the vine, which is Christ, and become again an intimate part of the Mystical Body, through penance and conversion and communion.

The only distinction that exists between Catholics on earth is one of function. Our Lord, as Saint Paul points out so clearly, selected men to be the ministers of His graces to others and to carry on the visible Church which He established. They were ordained to exercise His authority and to teach men to observe all things which Christ Our Lord commanded them.

The hierarchy and the clergy exist to serve all Catholics. Pope and Bishop and Priest are bound to believe in the same truths and practice and the same morality and receive the same sacraments as all Catholic men and women throughout the world.

Every Catholic, therefore, is the Catholic Church. Every Catholic, therefore, should be proud of his Church. Every Catholic can be proud of his Church, yesterday, today and forever. Every Catholic is united to every other Catholic, not merely to those who live today, but to those who lived in other days and who in the beautiful language of the Memento of the Dead at Mass "have gone before us with the sign of faith and who sleep the sleep of peace." This is the doctrine of the Communion of Saints.

Every Catholic then should know something of what those Catholics of other days did and thought. They were a part of bygone civilizations just as we are a part of our present civilization. A knowledge of their history will justify our love of them. The Church has nothing to fear from the truth. She has everything to fear from ignorance and prejudice.

To make the Church better known by all, Catholic and non-Catholic alike, and to make the Church better loved by those who are now a part of her, is the purpose of this volume.

May the blessing of Almighty God accompany these pages wherever they go. May the minds of those who read them be filled with light; their hearts, with love; their souls, with peace; and their lifetime, with Catholic Action.

REV. EDWARD LODGE CURRAN, PH.D.

21 Clinton Avenue
Brooklyn, N. Y.

June 13, 1938

Reverend Edward Lodge Curran, Ph.D.
President
International Catholic Truth Society
407 Bergen Street
Brooklyn, New York.

Dear Reverend Doctor:—

I take great pleasure in endorsing your selection and treatment of great moments in Catholic History. Every Catholic will derive profit and pleasure from reading your book.

To be Catholic, in every sense of the term, it is necessary for our people to have a true appreciation of the history of their Church. Most of our good people have no time to peruse the larger and more detailed volumes of Church History. For them the publication of the present volume is invaluable.

Your book should serve a most useful purpose as supplementary reading for the pupils in all our grade schools.

Even the scholar may refresh his memory of great events through the medium of this publication.

With the hope that your book may have a long and successful life, I remain

Sincerely yours,
(Signed) ✠ *Thomas E. Molloy*
Bishop of Brooklyn

To

THE REV. JOHN E. RYAN, A.M.

Of Cathedral College, Brooklyn, N. Y.

an old friend and a loyal friend
this book is affectionately
dedicated by the author.

The Annunciation

ON MARCH 25th of every year, Catholics all over the world celebrate the feast of the Annunciation.

We see a little town called Nazareth nestling in the mountains of Galilee. Within the town is the house where Mary lives. She is young and beautiful and holy. Many hours of the day she spends in prayer and meditation. She is espoused to an older man whose name is Joseph.

Suddenly, while she kneels in prayer, a heavenly light shines brightly across the threshold. Her visitor is the Archangel Gabriel, sent by God to announce to Mary that she is to become the mother of God.

The Archangel Gabriel begins to speak: "Hail, full of grace, the Lord is with thee" (Luke 1:28). Mary is worried at hearing these words. The Archangel hastens to announce his message.

"Fear not, Mary, for thou hast found grace with God."

"Behold thou shalt conceive in thy womb, and shalt bring forth a son; and thou shalt call His name Jesus." (Luke 1: 30-31)

In obedience to the will of God, Mary, the beautiful virgin of Galilee, gave her consent.

"And Mary said: Behold the handmaid of the Lord; be it done to me according to thy word. And the Angel departed from her" (Luke 1: 38).

Our Lord received His human nature from Mary, just as we receive our human nature from our own mothers. The Holy Ghost, however, and not Saint Joseph, begot Jesus in the womb of Mary.

The Blessed Virgin Mary is the greatest Catholic woman in the history of the world. We recall her Annunciation in the "Angelus" and in the "Hail Mary." The first part of the "Hail Mary" contains the words of the Angel. Another part contains the words which her cousin Saint Elizabeth used as a greeting when Mary visited her. The last part has been added by the Church.

"Hail Mary, full of grace; the Lord is with thee. (The Angel's words)

"Blessed art thou among women, and blessed is the fruit of thy womb, Jesus. (Saint Elizabeth's greeting) "Holy Mary, mother of God, pray for us sinners, now and at the hour of our death. Amen." (The Church's addition).

1

BETHLEHEM

CHRIST, Our Lord, founded the Catholic Church.

Therefore His birth is one of the most important events in the life of the Church. Our calendar is dated from the birth of Christ. The years before the birth of Christ are called B.C., "before Christ." The years after the birth of Christ are called A.D. from the Latin words, "anno Domini," meaning in the year of Our Lord. The word "Bethlehem" comes from two Hebrew words meaning "House of God."

"And it came to pass," as Saint Luke tells us, "that in those days there went out a decree from Caesar Augustus, that the whole world should be enrolled." (Luke 2:1)

Everyone was to be enrolled, or placed on the census list, in the town of his family. Therefore Mary and Joseph had to travel from Nazareth to Bethlehem, because they were both of the Jewish tribe of David, and Bethlehem was David's city.

When they reached the city, there was no room in the inns or hotels of Bethlehem.

Thus wandering they reached a stable outside the city. There were animals in the stable. There was also straw. And there Christ was born. Mary wrapped Him in swaddling clothes and laid Him in a manger. Saint Joseph, not the real father, but only the foster-father of Jesus, knelt in adoration, because the little infant lying in the manger was God as well as man. Mary always remained a virgin. Jesus was her only Son.

There, also, in the skies above, a heavenly army of angels sang out the Christmas message: "Glory to God in the highest; and on earth peace to men of good will." There from the surrounding fields that were bathed in silver the shepherds came to wonder and adore. There also, led by the star, the three Magi, or Kings from the East, gathered to give to Our Lord their gifts of gold and frankincense and myrrh.

No wonder a Catholic poet, Richard Crashaw wrote the following beautiful words about the divine Christ Child:

"Gloomy night embraced the place,
Where the noble Infant lay.
The Babe looked up and showed His face;
In spite of darkness, it was day.
It was thy day, Sweet; and did rise
Not from the East but from thine eyes."

2

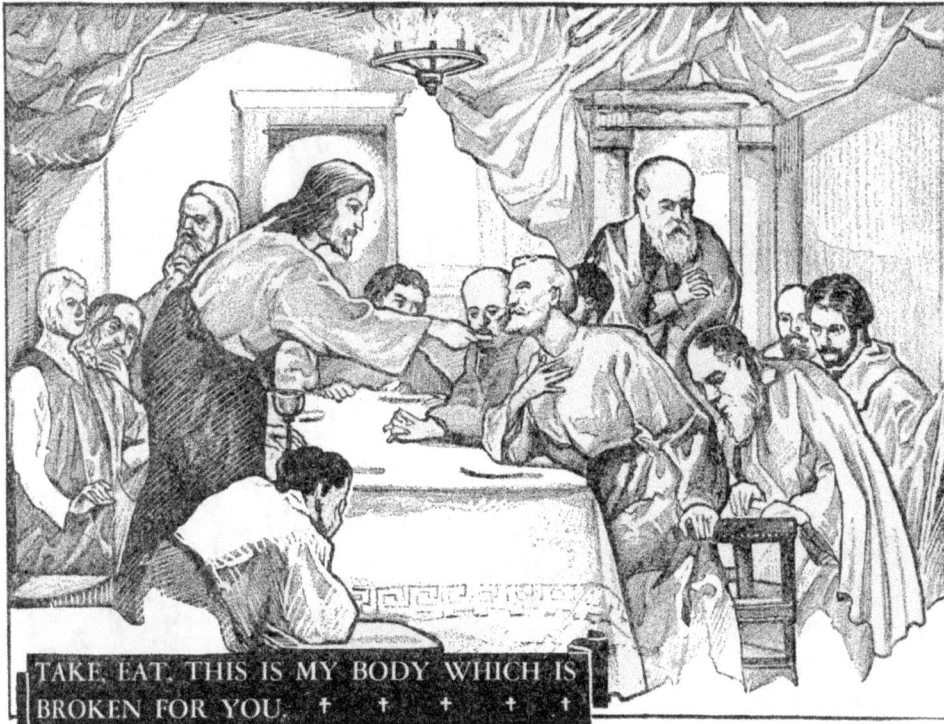

TAKE, EAT, THIS IS MY BODY WHICH IS BROKEN FOR YOU. † † † †

The Last Supper

WHEN Our Lord and Savior Jesus Christ was thirty years of age, He left His home in Nazareth, in order to preach to the people of Palestine.

For three years He proved to the world that He was God. These years are known as the public life of Our Lord.

One of the great annual feasts of the Jews is called the Pesach, or the Passover. During this religious ceremony a lamb was killed to recall the time that the Jews had been delivered by God from the cruel Egyptians.

The last supper which Our Lord had with His Apostles took place on the religious feast of the Passover. During this Last Supper Our Lord first celebrated Mass, first ordained the Apostles priests and bishops, and first gave them Holy Communion.

Whenever we attend Mass we see an altar and a priest. We also see people going up to the altar rail to receive Holy Communion. These things should remind us of what Our Lord said and did at the Last Supper nineteen hundred years ago.

"And taking bread, he gave thanks, and brake; and gave to them, saying: This is my body, which is given for you. Do this for a commemoration of me.

"In like manner the chalice also, after he had supped, saying: This is the chalice, the new testament in my blood, which shall be shed for you." (Luke 22 :19)

This is the Mass. The body and blood of Christ is offered up to God under the appearances of bread and wine, even as Christ did on the night of the last supper. Those who receive Holy Communion receive the body and blood, the soul and divinity of Our Lord and Savior Jesus Christ, even as the Apostles did at the Last Supper.

It was at the Last Supper, also, that Our Lord gave to the world a commandment of love.

"A new commandment I give unto you: that you love one another, as I loved you, that you also love one another." (John 23:34)

Our Lord has given Himself to us forever through Holy Communion. He wants the sacrifice of the Mass to be continued forever.

The Last Supper was the first Mass.

3

THE CRUCIFIXION

DURING His earthly life Our Lord went around doing good. Why, then, was He condemned to death?

Why did Our Lord have to take a cross upon His shoulders and die upon it between two thieves? What is meant by the words "Good Friday"?

Christ, Himself, told us why He died. He said that His blood would be shed for the remission of our sins. Christ died so that the punishment of Original Sin, the sin committed by our first parents, might be lifted from the world. That is why we call the day on which He died, "Good Friday."

When Christ was arrested by the Jews and brought before the High Priest Caiphas, He was accused of claiming to be God. The leaders of the Jewish religion were angered at Our Lord because He said He was God. Yet everything He said and did proved that He was truly God and truly man. The Jewish High Priest decided that Our Lord must die.

When, however, the same Jewish leaders brought Our Lord before Pontius Pilate, governor of Judea, they did not accuse Him of calling himself God.

They accused Our Lord of claiming to be King. Therefore, they said to Pilate, Christ is a traitor to Caesar and the Roman Government.

Our Lord assured Pilate that His Kingdom was not of this world. Our Lord said that His Kingdom was the Kingdom of God, and not an earthly Kingdom such as the Empire of Rome.

Pilate believed Our Lord. As it was the feast of the Passover, the Jews were entitled to have one prisoner pardoned. Pilate tried to have the Jews let Christ go free. Instead, the Jews chose to free Barabbas, a murderer, and to crucify Our Lord. Pilate then consented to His death.

Our Lord then traveled the trail of blood. We can follow this trail by means of the Fourteen Stations of the Cross that hang upon the walls of our parish church.

Three times Our Lord fell. Finally, He was nailed to the Cross. His blood dripped like rose petals upon the ground. At the end of three hours He died—for you and for me!

The Resurrection

THERE are three gardens in the history of the world which we must never forget. One is the Garden of Eden, where our first parents lived and where Original Sin was committed.

The second is the Garden of Gethsemani. There, the human nature of Our Lord suffered intense pain at the thought of the suffering He had to endure. There He sweat blood. There, also, Judas betrayed Him with a kiss.

The third is the Easter Garden, or the Garden of Resurrection. It is a fact that Our Lord arose from the dead. Our Lord's Resurrection is just as real as the discovery of America by Columbus or the winning of the American Revolution by George Washington.

After Our Lord's death Joseph of Arimathea asked Pilate for His body. Our Lord's body was taken down from the Cross, as we see in the Thirteenth Station of the Cross. It was wrapped in a long winding sheet, or shroud, and laid in Joseph of Arimathea's tomb, as we see in the Fourteenth Station of the Cross.

The Jews were permitted to place soldiers before the sepulchre. In addition, a huge stone had been rolled in place to close the entrance.

And early, Sunday morning, Mary Magdalen, whom Our Lord had converted, and two other women went to the sepulchre in order to anoint the body of Our Lord with spices.

Imagine their wonderment when they arrived and found the stone rolled back. Imagine their joy when a young man "sitting on the right side, clothed with a white robe" said to them:

"Be not affrighted; you seek Jesus of Nazareth, who was crucified: He is risen, He is not here. Behold the place where they laid Him." (Mark 16: 6)

They rushed back to tell the Apostles. While they were gone Our Lord revealed Himself to Mary Magdalen in the garden.

Later, Our Lord appeared in the upper chamber where the Apostles were gathered for fear of the Jews. He showed them the marks of the nail and spear wounds on His hands and His feet and His side to prove that He had really risen from the dead.

The Resurrection of Our Lord is the greatest proof of His divinity. Easter is the greatest feast in the calendar of the Church.

The Ascension

DURING the forty days after His Resurrection Our Lord appeared to the Apostles in the little upper chamber, where they were hiding from the Jews. "Peace be to you," He said. "As the Father sent me, I also send you.

"When He had said this, He breathed on them; and He said to them: Receive ye the Holy Ghost.

"Whose sins you shall forgive, they are forgiven them; and whose sins you shall retain (not forgive), they are retained (not forgiven)" (John 20: 21-23).

It was during those forty days, as we read in the Gospel of Saint Matthew, that Our Lord sent His Apostles forth to Christianize the world.

"Going therefore, teach ye all nations: baptizing them in the name of the Father and of the Son and of the Holy Ghost.

"Teaching them to observe all things whatsoever I have commanded you. And behold I am with you all days, even to the consummation of the world" (Matthew 28: 19-20).

Now the time to go was at hand. Saint Luke has described the beauty of the Ascension in the *Acts of the Apostles*. Once again Our Lord gathered together His Apostles and His Disciples. He spoke to them:

"And when He had said these things, while they looked on, He was raised up: and a cloud received Him out of their sight.

"And while they were beholding Him going up to heaven, behold two men stood by them in white garments.

"Who also said: Ye men of Galilee, why stand you looking up to heaven? This Jesus who is taken up from you into heaven shall so come as you have seen Him going into heaven." (Acts 1: 9-11)

Our Lord had gone. But He did not leave us alone. He left us the Catholic Church wherein we are safe and happy and secure.

The conversion of the world is the first and greatest form of Catholic Action. We must always believe the truths and obey the commandments of Our Lord and Savior Jesus Christ. He was born for us. He died for us. He ascended into heaven where we hope to be with Him when we die.

PENTECOST

THE Catholic feast of Pentecost, which occurs fifty days after Easter, recalls the descent of the Holy Ghost, upon the Apostles.

"And when the days of the Pentecost were accomplished, they were all together in one place:

"And suddenly there came a sound from heaven, as of a mighty wind coming, and it filled the whole house where they were sitting.

"And there appeared to them parted tongues as it were of fire, and it sat upon every one of them:

"And they were all filled with the Holy Ghost, and they began to speak with diverse tongues, according as the Holy Ghost gave them to speak." (Acts 11: 1-4) Imagine the Apostles gathered together in a dark- ened room. Their divine leader had returned to heaven. They feel fearful and alone. Suddenly, there is the sound of a mighty wind. A light appears above each head. It is a tongue of fire. Their souls are filled with the Holy Ghost.

Gone is their fear. Gone is their loneliness. The strength and power and presence of the Holy Ghost is within them. They rush out into the city.

The crowd stands in amazement. There are Jews from many lands: from Egypt, from the Island of Crete, from Rome, from Persia, from Mesopotamia. They speak different languages. Miraculously, they listen to the preaching of the Apostles and hear it, everyone, in his own tongue.

Saint Peter, the head of the Apostles, inspires the multitude with his words.

"Do penance," he says, "and be baptized every one of you in the name of Jesus Christ, for the remission of your sins: and you shall receive the gift of the Holy Ghost." (Acts 11: 38)

Three thousand are baptized and accept the truths of Christ. Three thousand become Catholics and dwell together in common, "persevering in the doctrine of the Apostles, and in the communication of the breaking of bread, and in prayers."

Thousands more are to become converts in the days and weeks and months and years and centuries to follow.

This day, when the Holy Ghost descended upon the Apostles and when Saint Peter spoke, is Pentecost, the birthday of the Catholic Church.

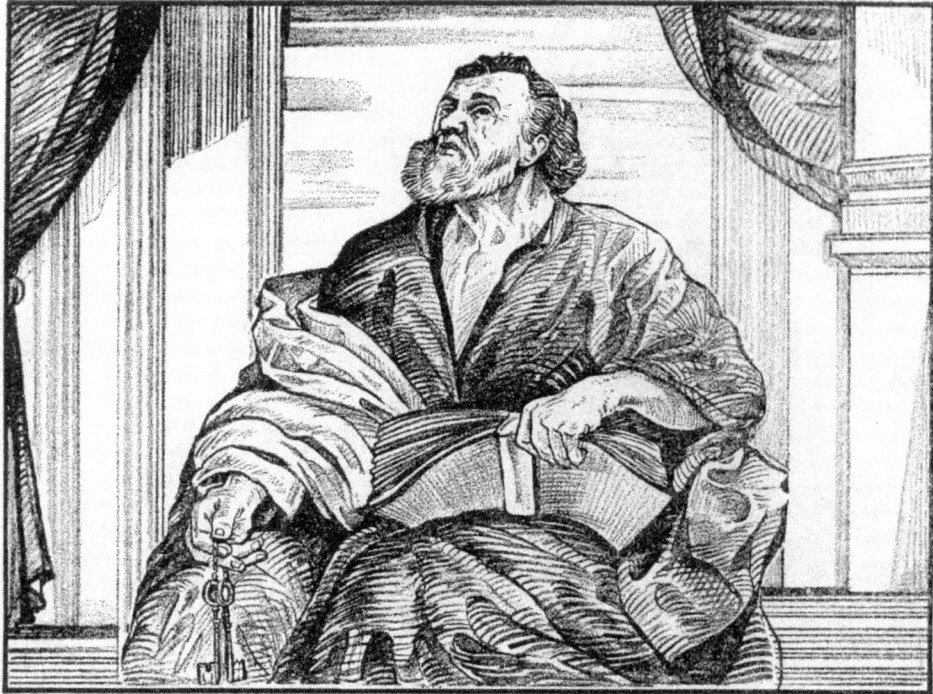

The First Pope

O N ONE occasion Our Lord asked His followers what men said about Him. The Disciples told Our Lord that some thought He was John the Baptist or the prophet Elias or the prophet Jeremias.

Then Our Lord asked the Apostles and Disciples what they thought about Him. Saint Peter immediately answered that Our Lord was God.

"Simon Peter answered and said: Thou art Christ, the Son of the Living God.

"And Jesus answering, said to him: Blessed art thou, Simon Bar-Jona (son of Jona): because flesh and blood hath not revealed it to thee, but my Father who is in heaven.

"And I say to thee: that thou art Peter, and upon this rock I will build my Church. And the gates of hell shall not prevail against it.

"And I will give to thee the keys of the kingdom of heaven. And whatsoever thou shalt bind upon earth, it shall be bound also in heaven: and whatsoever thou shalt loose on earth, it shall be loosed also in heaven." (Matthew 35: 16-19)

By these words Our Lord promised that Peter would be the visible head of His Church. Thus Peter became the first Pope.

Saint Peter's original name was Simon. It was Our Lord who called him Peter. Our Lord used the Greek word "*petra*" which means "rock."

Simon Peter was a Jew and a fisherman of the town of Bethsaida on the shores of Lake Genesareth. His brother Andrew was also one of the Apostles.

On the night of Our Lord's betrayal Peter became afraid and denied Him. He never stopped shedding bitter tears for the sin of his denial.

Saint Peter wrote two letters, or Epistles, in the New Testament. He brought the first Gentiles, non-Jewish converts, into the Church.

In Rome, during the persecution of the Emperor Nero (64-68 A.D.), Saint Peter was crucified. He made them place his head downward, towards the earth, to show that he was not worthy to be crucified like Our Lord.

The great *basilica* or Church of Saint Peter in Rome has been built over his tomb. Every visitor to Rome stops to pray at the tomb of Saint Peter, the first Pope.

"LORD, LAY NOT THIS SIN TO THEIR CHARGE"

The First Martyr

THE first martyr in the history of the Catholic Church was a man named Stephen. Like many other Jews Stephen was a convert to the Catholic Church. He later became a deacon.

The Apostles, who were Bishops, and the Priests, who assisted the Bishops, preached the truths of Our Lord and administered His Sacraments. From the very beginning, however, the Catholic Church collected money and goods and distributed them to the poor. To do this was the duty of the first deacons.

We read about Saint Stephen in a book of the New Testament which is called the *Acts of the Apostles.* The word "Acts" means deeds or activities.

While taking care of the needs of the Christian poor, Saint Stephen was also a great preacher. He told the people about Our Lord, about His Resurrection and about the Church which Our Lord had founded.

"And Stephen, full of grace and fortitude, did great wonders and signs among the people" (Acts 6: 8).

Saint Stephen was hated by the Jews. He was arrested and brought before the Jewish Council. Standing before the High Priest, Saint Stephen spoke about the wonderful favors which God had always bestowed upon the Jewish people. He also reproved them for persecuting Our Lord and Savior, Jesus Christ, just as their ancestors had persecuted the prophets.

His enemies were cut to the heart by his speech. They rushed upon him, dragged him outside the city and stoned him. Thus it was that Saint Stephen became the first martyr. The word "martyr" means a witness. It is used to describe those who have suffered death because they believed in the Faith.

As a deacon Saint Stephen was devoted to charity. He was charitable to the end. The last words of Saint Stephen were a prayer that God would forgive those who killed him.

"And falling on his knees, he cried with a loud voice, saying: Lord, lay not this sin to their charge" (Acts 7: 59).

Saint Stephen was the first among millions of Catholics who have died for the Faith of Our Lord.

We must always live for Our Lord. We must also be ready, if necessary, to die for Him.

9

CONVERSION OF SAINT PAUL

SAINT PAUL was the greatest missionary in the history of the Catholic Church. He was born in the Roman city of Tarsus. He was a Jew of the tribe of Benjamin. Saul was his Jewish name. Paul was his Roman name. He was present when the Jews stoned Saint Stephen, the first martyr.

He went from synagogue to synagogue spying on those Jews who had become Christians and reporting them to the Jewish Council.

One day Saul set out for the town of Damascus. He intended to arrest any Jews in Damascus who had become Christians and to bring them bound to Jerusalem.

"And as he went on his journey, it came to pass that he drew nigh to Damascus. And suddenly a light from heaven shined round about him.

"And falling on the ground, he heard a voice saying to him: Saul, Saul, why persecutest thou me?

"Who said: Who art thou, Lord? And He: I am Jesus whom thou persecutest. It is hard for thee to kick against the goad.

"And he, trembling and astonished, said: Lord, what wilt Thou have me to do?

"And the Lord said to him: Arise and go into the city; and there it shall be told thee what thou must do. Now the men who went in company with him stood amazed, hearing indeed a voice but seeing no man.

"And Saul arose from the ground: and when his eyes were opened, he saw nothing. But they, leading him by the hands, brought him to Damascus" (Acts 9: 3-8).

In Damascus Our Lord sent a Christian called Ananias to Saul. Ananias was at first afraid to go. But the Lord said to Ananias:

"Go thy way: for this man is to me a vessel of election, to carry my name before the Gentiles and kings and the children of Israel" (Acts 9: 15).

Ananias feared no longer. He came to Saul and placed his hands upon him and instructed him. Saul was baptized. His sight returned. Henceforth he used only the name of Paul.

"And immediately he preached Jesus in the synagogues, that He is the son of God" (Acts 9: 20).

The Jews of Damascus planned to kill him, but Saint Paul escaped and became the greatest missionary in the Christian world.

The Greatest Missionary

THE name "Christian" was first given to the followers of Our Lord in the city of Antioch. In the year 45 Saint Paul and Saint Barnabas left Antioch on their first missionary journey, 45-49 A.D., through the pagan world.

From Antioch to the island of Cyprus and from Cyprus to the cities of Asia Minor they went. They preached first to the Jews in their synagogues and later to the Gentiles.

"To you," Saint Paul said to the Jews, "it behooved us first to speak the word of God; but because you reject it, and judge yourselves unworthy of eternal life, behold we turn to the Gentiles."

Three times Saint Paul traveled through the Mediterranean world: 45-49 A.D.; 51-54 A.D. and 54-58 A.D. In Athens Saint Paul once cried out: "Ye men of Athens, I perceive that in all things you are too superstitious. For passing by and seeing your idols, I found an altar also on which was written: To the Unknown God. What therefore you worship, without knowing it, that I preach to you."

Because of his preaching the people of Ephesus in Asia Minor abandoned their worship of the goddess Diana. In vain the silversmiths, who profited by the silver statues they made of Diana, tried to overcome him.

Wherever he went, he left a Catholic congregation. Thirteen letters, or Epistles, were written by Saint Paul to these congregations.

At the end of his last journey the Jews of Jerusalem had him arrested and confined to prison. As a Roman citizen he appealed to the court of Caesar. He was sent to Rome.

There in the midst of the persecution of the Christians by Nero, in the year 64 A.D., Saint Paul was beheaded.

He had finally won the crown of justice of which he wrote to Saint Timothy: "The time of my dissolution is at hand. I have fought a good fight, I have finished my course, I have kept the faith. As to the rest, there is laid up for me a crown of justice, which the Lord the just judge will render to me in that day; and not only to me, but to them also that love His coming."
(II Timothy 4 :6-8)

LAST OF THE APOSTLES

THERE are always two Gospels read in every Catholic Mass. The first Gospel is read as soon as the priest passes from the right of the altar, the Epistle side, to the left or Gospel side. The second, or last Gospel, is read in the same place just before the priest descends the steps to say the prayers at the close of Mass.

This last Gospel is generally the Gospel of Saint John. It consists of the first fourteen verses of the first chapter of the Gospel written by Saint John. It tells us how Our Lord was God and united with His Father from all eternity. It tells us in simple language that all can understand how the Jews refused to believe in the divinity of Our Lord.

"He was in the world: and the world was made by Him: and the world knew Him not.

"He came unto His own: and His own received Him not" (John 1:10-11).

Saint John wrote his Gospel sometime between the years 80 and 100 A.D. Saint John always preached about the divinity of Our Lord. Therefore, he has become known as Saint John the Divine.

Saint John was the brother of Saint James, and like his brother, a fisherman.

He was always very close to Our Lord. It was Saint John who sat next to Our Lord at the Last Supper. It was Saint John who stood at the foot of the Cross. It was Saint John to whom Our Lord bequeathed the care of His Blessed Mother, when He died.

From the very beginning of his life with Our Lord, Saint John was known as the Beloved Disciple.

During the persecution of the Roman Emperor Domitian (95-96 A.D.) Saint John was plunged into a caldron of boiling oil but miraculously escaped any harm. He was banished to the island of Patmos, where he wrote the last book of the New Testament, known as the Apocalypse.

When he returned to the city of Ephesus, he wrote his Gospel and the three Epistles, or letters, which bear his name.

We must never forget the commandment of love which the beloved Disciple of Our Lord kept repeating:

"Little children, love one another."

The First Council

THE word "Council" means a gathering of people for the purpose of discussing something. A Church Council means a gathering of Bishops and priests called together by the Pope or with the approval of the Pope.

The first Council held by the Catholic Church was the Council of Jerusalem. It was held around the year 50 A.D. (Acts 15: 6-21).

Part of the name of "Jerusalem" comes from the Hebrew word "Salim" which means "peace." The city was originally called Salem. The purpose of the Council of Jerusalem was to bring about peace.

The first converts to the Catholic Church were Jews. The Apostles all were of the Jewish race. Our Lord Himself, as man, had chosen to be born of a Jewish mother, the Blessed Virgin.

But Our Lord did not intend that His truths should be taught only to the Jewish people. Everyone was invited to become a member of His Church.

Saint Peter had brought the Gentile Cornelius, the Roman captain, into the Church. On his missionary journeys Saint Paul preached to both Jews and Gentiles.

The word "Gentile" was used in the Old Testament to describe all people who were not of the Jewish race.

After his first missionary journey, Saint Paul reported how many Gentiles had become members of the Catholic Church. Some of the Jewish Catholics in Antioch in Asia Minor insisted that the Gentile-Catholics should also follow the customs of the Jews.

Saint Paul and his friend Barnabas objected. They went to Jerusalem. There the Apostles met under the leadership of Saint Peter, the first Pope.

The Council of Jerusalem decided that the Gentile-Converts would not have to become Jews in order to become Catholics. This decision was made by Saint Peter, who was a Jew, and by the Apostles, who were also Jews.

Saint Peter, the first Pope, and the Apostles, the first Bishops, remained true to the command of Christ. Our Lord established only one Church. All nations were to belong to it. Gentiles and Jews by becoming Catholics became brothers in Christ.

The Gentile did not have to become a Jew. The Jew did not have to become a Gentile. Both had to become Christians.

Ten Persecutions

THIRTY years after the death and resurrection and ascension of Our Lord, the Roman Empire began to persecute the Church.

The Roman Empire consisted of a few people who were free and wealthy and of many people who were slaves. The Catholic Church taught that every human being was equal in the sight of God. Every man had a soul created by God and redeemed by the Precious Blood of Our Lord. Since the Roman Empire was based on slavery it hated this teaching of the Catholic Church.

The Roman Emperor also claimed to be God. He made all citizens worship him. He demanded that all people offer religious sacrifices to him and the pagan gods of Rome. Catholics refused to do so.

Dragged unjustly before the courts, even as Our Lord was dragged before the Courts of Caiphas, the High Priest and Pilate, the Roman Governor, Catholics refused to give up their belief in Christ and their loyalty to the Church. Therefore they were tortured and put to death.

Many of them were huddled together in large arenas, like the Coliseum. Cages containing wild and starving lions were placed along the sides. The Emperor himself, his court and all the fine men and ladies of Roman society, as well as the people of Rome, crowded the benches. The doors were opened. The lions rushed forth to devour the Christians. Singing hymns and uttering prayers, even prayers of forgiveness for their enemies, they gave their blood to the sand and their souls to God. These were the first Christian martyrs.

For the first three hundred years of Christianity these persecutions went on with increasing fury. Ten official persecutions by the following Roman Emperors tried their best to destroy the Church.

1. Nero (64–68)
2. Domitian (94–96)
3. Trajan (98-117)
4. Marcus Aurelius (166–180)
5. Septimius Severus (202–211)
6. Maximinus Thrax (235–238)
7. Decius (249–251)
8. Valerian (247–259)
9. Aurelian (270–275)
10. Diocletian (284–305)

Neither the sword nor the torch nor the wild beasts nor the horrors of prison could make the early Christians give up their faith. They loved Our Lord and His Church.

The early martyrs suffered and triumphed. The Church was saved. We must always remember the words of Our Lord and the lives of the martyrs.

The Catacombs

THE word "subway" makes us think of a flight of stairs which takes us down below the surface of the earth to a platform.

The Catacombs were like subways in Rome. They were built by the Christians who lived during the first three hundred years after Our Lord's death. Down a long stairway the early Christians went, from 30 to 50 feet beneath the surface of the earth. At the end of the stairway was a passageway or gallery, just wide enough for a person to walk through. The roof of the gallery was ten or thirteen feet high.

The air was cool and damp. Other passageways branched off from the main one. Openings in the walls led to rooms or chambers. There were slabs of marble or of tile along the sides of the passageways and on the walls of the rooms.

These Catacombs, or subways, are the last resting place of the early Christians. They were buried in the walls of the passageways and rooms. Two million graves are in the Catacombs of Rome.

The writings on the walls are particularly tender and beautiful. "Sweet Simplicius, live in eternity" is the last wish which those who buried Simplicius wrote upon his grave.

On another grave, in the Catacomb of Domitilla, unmarked by any name, is the beautiful prayer: "May thy spirit be in refreshment."

From the names of those who are buried in the Catacombs we read that the rich as well as the poor, the powerful as well as the humble, became Catholics during the first three hundred years of Christianity. The bodies of the poor lie side by side with the rich, their dust joined together in this life even as we hope that their souls are joined together in the life to come.

When the persecutions ceased, no more Catacombs were built. In 410 A.D. a German tribe known as the Goths captured Rome and destroyed a large part of it. For many centuries the Catacombs were forgotten.

Three hundred years ago Catholic and non-Catholic scholars began to study these ancient burial places. The Catholics of the first three hundred years had the same faith, the same hope and the same love as we have.

May they rest in peace!

Constantine The Great

CONSTANTINE THE GREAT (275-337 A.D.) was born in Serbia. His father was Constantius, a Roman officer, who became Emperor of Rome in 305. His mother was Saint Helena.

At the time of his father's death Constantine was with the Roman army in Britain. The popularity and bravery of Constantine made him loved by the men of the army, captains as well as spearmen. With great shouts and cheering the soldiers selected him to succeed his father as Emperor of Rome. His brother-in-law, Licinius, was already Emperor in Constantinople.

Constantine immediately marched towards Rome in order to take over his position as Emperor. Meanwhile a man named Maxentius, the wicked son of Maximian, one of the cruelest emperors who ever persecuted the Church, proclaimed that he was Emperor of Rome.

Northern Italy hailed Constantine as Emperor. He then marched against the army of Maxentius. Suddenly, on the march, Constantine fixed his eyes upon the sky. A strange sight appeared before him. He saw a Cross. On the Cross he saw some Latin words: "In Hoc Signo Vinces."

He was not far from Rome. He was near the Milvian bridge, where the troops of Maxentius were waiting to destroy him and prevent him from becoming Emperor. The message of the Cross caused him to proceed courageously. He no longer feared. His tired troops became inspired. "In this sign," said the Cross, "thou shalt conquer."

Pledging his loyalty to the Cross, which he recognized as the Cross of Christ, Constantine marched on to defeat the troops of Maxentius. By the battle of the Milvian Bridge, October 28, 312, Constantine the Great became Roman Emperor in the West.

He had marched beneath the Cross of Christ and conquered. Other emperors had tried to destroy the Cross and were themselves destroyed. The victory of Constantine brought freedom and peace to the Catholic Church.

Constantine read and studied. He did not hasten his conversion. Towards the close of his life, he was baptized and received into the Church by Pope Sylvester I.

The Cross of Christ had conquered for Constantine at the Milvian Bridge. In the sign of the Cross we Catholics can conquer everything in life.

EDICT OF MILAN

IT WAS at Milan, over fifteen hundred years ago, that a Roman Emperor, called Constantine the Great, declared the freedom of the Christian Church. This was in the year 313 A.D.

Up to that time every Roman Emperor had done his best to destroy Christianity. Every possible torture was used to make people give up their belief in Our Lord.

After three hundred years, the Roman Emperors admitted that all their attempts had ended in failure. Evidently, the Christian religion was from God. It could not be destroyed by human means. If Christianity were only human, it would have been destroyed long ago.

In the beginning of the fourth century, then, the Roman Emperors began to change their attitude towards the Christians. One of them, named Galerius, who died in 311, even asked the Christians to pray to their God for him and his successors.

A Roman Emperor, who was supposed to be a god, had finally admitted that the ruler of the entire universe was greater than himself. Christ, Our Lord, had conquered.

A new Emperor now appeared in the West. His name was Constantine. Constantine decided to allow the Christians to worship God as they wished. He permitted them to buy property and to build beautiful churches.

Constantine announced this decision at Milan, in 313 A.D. It has come to be known as the Edict of Milan. The prayers which Galerius had asked the Christians to say were bearing fruit!

Recognition of Christianity and the end of the persecutions meant Christian peace for the Roman empire. The Church was now able to come up from the Catacombs and worship Our Lord in public.

The Edict of Milan provided that each man could follow his own religion without any interference on the part of the government. Freed from persecution and rescued from the Catacombs, Christianity attracted all people by the truth of its doctrines, the purity of its morals and the beauty of its ceremonies.

The martyrs who had died for Our Lord had not died in vain. That is why the blood of martyrs is called the seed of the Church. The Edict of Milan had conquered all former edicts of persecution.

17

Council of Nicea

EVERY Sunday, after the priest has finished reading the Gospel in Latin at the left side of the altar, he returns to the middle of the altar and calls out, "Credo in unum Deum." This means, "I believe in one God." Then, in a lower voice, he continues to recite what is known as the Nicene Creed.

We know that the Apostles' Creed comes from the time of the Apostles. The Apostles' Creed is a brief statement of the main truths which every Catholic must believe.

The Nicene Creed contains the same truths as the Apostles' Creed. The Nicene Creed merely explains in more detail some of the truths contained in the Apostles' Creed. This creed derives its name from a certain city called Nicaea in Asia Minor. There, in the year 325, Pope St. Sylvester called for a meeting of all the Bishops of the Church.

The Catholic Church has always taught that Christ is God. Our Lord is just as much God as God the Father or God the Holy Ghost. Some men, however, tried to say that Our Lord was greater than man, but not God.

This false teaching, which denied the divinity of Our Lord, was a heresy. It was taught by a man called Arius. It is called Arianism. The purpose of the Council of Nicaea was to show the error of Arianism and to assure all Catholics that Our Lord was really and truly God. St. Athanasius disputed with Arius in a debate that is famous in history, and defeated him.

The Council of Nicaea likewise decided that the feast of Easter should be celebrated on the first Sunday after the spring full moon. The Bishop of Alexandria, who was an astronomer, was ordered to find out the date of Easter for several years to come. Because the full moon does not come at the same time every year, the date of Easter, as we know, changes each year.

Arius refused to accept the teachings of the Church. He became a heretic. A heretic is a person who believes in some but not all the truths taught by Our Lord. The Council of Nicaea declared that no one who rejects the divinity of Our Lord can remain a Catholic.

The True Cross

THE True Cross refers to the Cross on which Our Blessed Lord and Savior died for the salvation of the world.

In the fourth century, Saint Helena, mother of the Emperor Constantine, discovered it in Jerusalem. She sent part of it to Rome.

Both Saint Helena and the Emperor Constantine built two magnificent churches in Jerusalem to commemorate the discovery. One was built on the site of the Holy Sepulchre. The other was built on the site of Calvary and completed in the year 335 A.D.

On May the third we celebrate the Finding of the True Cross by Saint Helena. On September fourteenth of every year we celebrate the feast known as the Exaltation of the True Cross.

That part of the True Cross preserved in Jerusalem was later taken by the Persians. In the year 629 A.D. an eastern Roman Emperor, named Heraclius, recovered it from the Persians. We also celebrate this fact on September the fourteenth.

The Church has always preserved the relics of her Saints.

A relic may be a part of a Saint's body. Or it may be something which he used in life, such as an article of clothing or tools.

It is natural for us to preserve something which our mother used during life. We treat our mother's watch, for instance, with respect and love. The watch helps us to remember and love our mother.

In the same way we venerate or honor the relics of Saints. We do not worship them.

There are many particles of the True Cross preserved throughout the world. They are very small. They are very precious.

We do not possess all the fragments of the True Cross. Added together, all the relics of the True Cross in the world would not make up more than one-third of the Cross on which Our Lord died.

On Good Friday we sing the following beautiful hymn to remind us of Christ's Holy Cross:

Faithful Cross, above all others,
   One and only noble Tree,
None in foliage, none in blossom,
   None in fruit thy peer may be;
Sweetest Wood, and sweetest Iron;
   Sweetest weight is hung on thee.

The End of Paganism

IN THE year 313 A.D. the Emperor Constantine gave the Church her freedom. In the middle of the fourth century an Emperor named Julian abandoned the Church. He is known as Julian the Apostate (331-363 A.D.). An apostate is one who gives up all his faith. He tried to restore paganism as the religion of Rome. He died in the attempt. Wounded unto death Julian the Apostate took a handful of his own blood, threw it towards the sky and said: "O Galilean, thou hast conquered."

No man had more to do with the victory of Christianity than the great Saint Ambrose. Saint Ambrose's father was the Roman governor of the Roman province known as Gaul. Saint Ambrose was born in the city of Trier in 340 A.D. He became governor of northern Italy. He died in 397 A.D.

While he was studying to become a Catholic, the Bishop of Milan, in northern Italy, died. The people of Milan demanded that Ambrose become their Bishop. In obedience to the will of God Ambrose was baptized, confirmed, ordained a priest and consecrated a Bishop in 374 A.D. He then gave all his possessions to the poor.

Saint Ambrose fought against paganism with all his might. In 392 A.D. Theodosius, Emperor, forbade all worship of the pagan gods throughout the Empire. By the year 423 A.D. the Emperor Theodosius II declared that there were no longer any pagans in the Empire.

Saint Ambrose was a great defender of charity as well as a great defender of the Faith. When the Emperor Theodosius I massacred the population of Thessalonica, Saint Ambrose reproved the Emperor for his cruelty. He threatened to excommunicate the Emperor if he failed to repent. Theodosius obeyed and repented.

In memory of Saint Ambrose one of the great Catholic libraries of the world has been named the Ambrosian Library, in Milan. It was in this library that Pope Pius XI spent the greater part of his priestly life.

Saint Ambrose was a Bishop, a composer of hymns and a friend of the people. Through his effort Christianity, the religion of faith and hope and love, finally conquered paganism, which was a religion of doubt, despair and hatred.

SAINT AUGUSTINE

IT WAS from the sweet voice of our mothers that we first learned about God, about the Church, about the Sacraments, about doing good and avoiding evil.

This has been the life of every Catholic mother in the world. It was, therefore, the daily life of a noble mother named Saint Monica who lived in the city of Tagaste, northern Africa, centuries ago. There she had married a pagan Roman called Patricus. There she had given birth to a very strong and intelligent son whom she named Augustine (354-430 A.D.).

When her son grew up she taught him all the things which we learned from the lips of our mothers. But like many other sons and daughters, Augustine began to associate with bad companions. In the city of Carthage, where he went to study law, he lived a life which caused his mother to weep with sorrow. He refused to follow her example.

And still his mother, the Catholic Saint Monica, prayed for him. Her prayers followed him to Carthage. Her prayers followed him to Italy, where, in the year 383 A.D., he taught school in the city of Milan.

In Milan the prayers of Saint Monica were answered. Her son Augustine met and heard the saintly Bishop Ambrose.

After years of penance and study he was baptized by Saint Ambrose in 387 A.D. The next year he returned to his native city of Tagaste. In expiation of his wickedness he gave all that he possessed to the poor.

In 391 A.D. he became a priest. Five years later the people insisted that he become Bishop of the town of Hippo. And there for thirty-four years he defended the Church against all those who tried to attack her.

He wrote many books. One, called his "*Confessions*," was written to warn others of the dangers and evils of sin. Another, called the "*City of God*," was written to prove the truth of the Catholic Church.

In 387 Saint Monica died. She asked her son Augustine to pray for her every day and especially to offer Mass for her.

Her prayers for him had made her a Saint. Her prayers for him had also made him a Saint.

Saint Jerome and the Bible

IN THE time of Saint Augustine another very saintly man lived in the East. His name was Jerome (340-420 A.D.). Like Saint Augustine, Saint Jerome was also a great scholar. When he returned from his studies in Rome, he retired to the desert of Chalcis where from 374 to 379 he gave himself up to a life of prayer and solitude.

In obedience to the voice of God, Jerome returned to the city of Antioch and became a priest. There he met another Saint called Saint Gregory Nazianzus. Saint Gregory encouraged Saint Jerome to make a deep study of the Bible.

Although he was over forty years old, Saint Jerome began to study the original languages in which the Bible was written. He became a master of Hebrew and of Greek. He paid a visit to Rome where he became a friend of Pope Damasus I. Pope Damasus was anxious to have the Bible translated into Latin so that all the people might read it easily. For, by this time, Latin had become the popular language in the civilized world.

In obedience to the Pope, Jerome visited the Holy Land. There in Bethlehem the great scholar and Saint wrote the Latin edition of the Bible which is called the *Vulgate,* or popular edition. The Latin word "vulgus" means "people." This is the official copy used by the Church in all her ceremonies and in all her writings. This popular Latin edition was made over fifteen hundred years ago. From it we get our Douay Version, or English translation.

The Catholic Church has preserved the Bible for the past nineteen hundred years. Without her the Bible might have been lost in the midst of the barbarian invasions. When we hear the priest recite the Latin of the Mass we should be glad that Saint Jerome translated the Bible into Latin.

The Catholic Church has kept every book and every word of the Bible, because the Bible is the inspired word of God. The Catholic Church has always urged her members to read the Bible every day.

The Catholic Church is filled with the presence of the Holy Ghost. The Catholic Church has always loved the Bible. She alone has preserved it for the world.

Leo The Great Saves Rome

MANY times the Christian civilization of the world has been threatened with destruction. Today evil forces from Soviet Russia threaten to destroy it. Again and again, the Church has had to save civilization.

In the time of Pope Saint Leo the Great (440- 461 A.D.), word came to Rome that the Huns under Attila, "The Scourge of God," were on their way southward. The citizens of Italy were terrified. His troops had been defeated in France, at the town of Chalons on the river Marne. A Roman general, named Aetius, had turned him back after a fierce battle.

The "Scourge of God" was infuriated. He would have his revenge on Rome. As a barbarian he hated civilization. Schools and homes and farms and works of art would be destroyed.

Over the Alps Attila swept with his horsemen and footsoldiers. The bodies of men and women slaughtered in northern Italy were the only things left in the towns which he took and destroyed.

The citizens of Venetia abandoned their town and fled to some islands in the Adriatic sea. There, out of their fishing villages, the modern beautiful city of Venice arose.

On and on, nearer to Rome, killing men and women and children, destroying buildings, burning farms, Attila, the "Scourge of God," at last came face to face with Pope Leo, the Vicar of Christ, in Mantua.

The face of Attila was cruel. The face of Pope Leo was kindly. Around Attila were thousands of his warriors armed with their swords of conquest. Around Leo were a few Christian citizens from Rome, armed with the truth of Christ.

The man of war looked and listened to the man of peace. Strange words of Christ, the Prince of Peace, broke upon the ears of Attila. "All that take the sword shall perish with the sword."

He shuddered as he heard how not even the Roman Emperors were able to destroy Christianity. The shouts of his warriors died out. His eyes grew wide with wonderment.

There were other countries he could conquer. He gave his orders. He marched away—back to the north and east from whence he came. Pope Leo had conquered. Once again Christianity had saved civilization from the destroyer.

Fall of the Western Empire

IN THE time of Our Lord the Roman Empire stretched all around the Mediterranean Sea. On the north was Europe. On the east was Palestine. On the south was northern Africa. On the west were Spain and Morocco looking at each other across the Straits of Gibraltar.

The only civilized government in Europe was the government of Rome. Beyond the Roman cities and the Roman provinces German barbarians fought among themselves. They built no schools. They established no cities like those of the Roman Empire.

Again and again, however, these roving tribes of Germans tried to pass into Italy and overthrow the civilization of Rome. The Empire of Rome had preserved the civilization of Greece and Babylon and Egypt and Persia. The German invaders from the north were only interested in plundering cities and destroying farms. They were not interested in preserving anything.

Instead of growing strong, the pagan Roman Empire allowed her pagan citizens to become weak through vice and immorality. Contrary to the teaching of the Church the Roman Empire kept the vast majority of its citizens as slaves. Italy was filled with anarchy and

civil war. Ambitious generals fought with one another to become Emperor. When they became Emperors, they became tyrants.

When the persecutions came to an end in 313 A.D. the Catholic Church tried to do her best to preserve the civilization of Rome. She taught men to be virtuous. She taught men to be loyal to their country. She tried to abolish slavery. But the persecutions and the corruption of pagan Roman society were too deeply embedded.

In the end the barbarian troops from the north conquered. In 476 A.D. a German soldier, named Odoacer, killed the last Roman Emperor, named Romulus. No other emperor in the west succeeded him. Soon the Emperor in Constantinople abandoned the western Empire completely.

During the 150 years, from 313 to 476 A.D., the Church had done her best to strengthen the morals and the loyalty of the Roman Empire. Roman society however refused to heed her teachings and her warnings.

The Empire fell. A new task awaited the Church. The new tribes, which destroyed the Empire, had to be civilized and converted.

24

SAINT BENEDICT AND THE MONKS

FOR the first four hundred years of her existence the Catholic Church worked hard to Christianize the ancient world. She was persecuted in every way. Yet, she succeeded in conquering the paganism of ancient Rome.

At that moment barbarian tribes from northern and central Europe descended upon Italy. Education was destroyed. Farms were wasted. By the year 500 A.D. civilization itself seemed at an end.

Once again God raised up a valiant leader for His cause. In 480 A.D. Saint Benedict was born in the Roman city of Nursia. His father had destined him for a brilliant life in the world. The world, however, disgusted him. In the year 500 A.D. he took refuge in a narrow mountain cave near the town of Subiaco in Italy.

There, like every Saint of God, he spent his time in prayer and meditation. There, also, he instructed all who came to him. Within a short time twelve monasteries were established by Saint Benedict. He himself later withdrew to his monastery on Monte Cassino. There he died in the year 543 A.D.

The monastic rule, or way of living, established by Saint Benedict is one of the wonders of the world.

The monks took vows of poverty and chastity and obedience. In addition, they gathered together eight times a day to worship God by prayer. The rest of the time had to be spent in labor.

Some of the monks spent long hours copying the literature of the ancient world which the barbarians had almost destroyed. Others cultivated the fields and taught the peasants how to take care of their lands. Others founded schools and became teachers. Others devoted their lives to preaching. Wherever a Benedictine Monastery was founded, civilization as well as Christianity returned to Europe.

For hundreds of years the followers of Saint Benedict worked everywhere. Their labors were not in vain. From the sixth to the fourteenth century the Benedictines gave to the world twenty-four Popes, two hundred Cardinals, seven thousand Archbishops, fifteen thousand Bishops and over fifteen hundred Saints.

It was the monks of Saint Benedict who preserved civilization in Europe. Each monastery was a center of agriculture, and learning and holiness. The Benedictines have been a Benediction to the world.

Conversion of England

ABOUT thirteen hundred and fifty years ago a man named Gregory lived in Rome (540-604 A.D.). When he became thirty-four years of age, he decided to leave the world and to become a Benedictine monk.

One day, while he was walking through the streets of Rome, Gregory stopped. A group of strange young men stood in the market place near him. Their hair was blond instead of black. Their skin was fair instead of bronze. They were tall and strong. Their blue eyes looked courageously into his.

"Who are these young men?" Gregory asked. "They are Angles, youths from England, from the land of the Angles and Saxons." "No," said Gregory, "they are not Angles; they are Angels."

A few years later, in 590 A.D., Gregory became Pope on the death of Pelagius II. Messengers from the north brought happy news from England. A new King in England, Athelbert of Kent, had united nearly all of England under his power. Bertha, the wife of Athelbert, was a Catholic. The English were eager to hear about Christ and the Catholic Church.

Pope Gregory selected forty Benedictine monks and placed them under the leadership of a monk called Augustine. In June of the year 596 A.D. they set forth over mountain and valley and stream, until they reached southern France. In the spring of 597 they sailed from Boulogne and landed at Thanet.

A dozen miles away from Canterbury, the city of the King, Augustine and Athelbert met face to face. The King welcomed the little band of missionaries. He gave them a house in Canterbury and permitted them to preach as much as they wanted.

In a short time King Athelbert himself became a Catholic. The wonderful holiness of the monks and the clearness of their teaching moved thousands to become Catholics.

Augustine became the first Archbishop of Canterbury. As the number of Catholics grew, the kingdom of Athelbert was divided into dioceses, just as the United States of America is divided into dioceses and archdioceses today. Within fifty years after the coming of Augustine the English had become Catholics.

Because of Pope Saint Gregory and Saint Augustine many Angles (or English) became angels of learning and holiness throughout the history of England.

Saint Gregory the Great

THE loveliest title borne by the Popes of Rome is "Servus servorum Dei," the Latin words for "Servant of the Servants of God." The first Pope to use this beautiful title was Pope Saint Gregory I, who is also known as Gregory the Great.

At the time of Gregory the Great, a German tribe called the Lombards had settled in northern Italy. It was this tribe which has given the name of Lombardy to the northern part of Italy today.

Again and again they descended upon the city of Rome, leaving bloodshed and ruin as they marched. Again and again it was Gregory the Great who saved the people of Rome from destruction. It was he who helped the Romans rebuild the walls of their city.

Not until the Lombard King Agiluf became a Catholic did the invasions of the Lombards stop. In his work of converting the Lombards, Pope Saint Gregory received constant assistance from the Catholic wife of King Agiluf. She helped the Pope build the monastery of Bobbio in northern Italy. She also built the basilica of Saint John the Baptist near Milan.

There on the altar King Agiluf placed the iron crown of the Lombards to show his obedience to the Pope. This was the crown which Pope Leo III used at the coronation of Charlemagne, nearly three centuries later.

As a Benedictine monk Pope Saint Gregory I was devoted to learning. Nearly 850 letters, written by the Pope, have been left. Many of his sermons on the Gospels are in the Roman Breviary. The Breviary contains the official prayers which every priest must say every day.

In his book called the "Pastoral Rule" Gregory wrote about the qualities which every priest must possess in order to do the work of God. In his "Dialogues" Gregory recounted the saintly lives of many who lived in his time.

Gregory devoted an entire book to the life of Saint Benedict. He also explained the holy rule or way of living which Saint Benedict had laid down for his monks.

In the sixth century Pope Gregory I was a light shining in the darkness. The word "Great" is not too great to describe him.

CONVERSION OF IRELAND

IRELAND, or Eire, as it is called in the Gaelic language, has always been one of the most devoutly Catholic countries in Europe.

Ireland was converted by Saint Patrick (387-493 A.D.). In 433 A.D. Saint Patrick landed with his companions at Wicklow. For sixty years until his death in 493 he labored among the Irish.

When Patrick was only sixteen years of age he had been sent to Ireland as a slave. After six years he escaped and returned to Gaul, or France. There he studied. He was trained by Saint Germaine of Auxerre to be a missionary. The face of Ireland remained fixed upon his memory. He wanted to go back.

This time, with the permission of Pope Saint Celestine I, he went back, not as a slave but as a Bishop.

On Easter Sunday in the year 433 A.D. he stood before King Leoghaire. He spoke of Christ and the reason for His sufferings. He told of heaven, a place more beautiful than even the Irish lakes and hills. Stooping down he took a shamrock from the grass— one stem with three leaves—and showed it to them, to help them understand the mystery of the Trinity.

Up and down the length and breadth of Connaught he preached. He built many churches. He ordained many priests. From Connaught to Ulster; from Ulster to Meath; from Meath to Leinster; from Leinster to Munster—on and on he went, never tired, always strong and gay.

Twelve times he and his companions were taken and condemned to death. But God spared him until he became a very old man. Not until every part of Ireland had been converted did he die.

Queen Elizabeth and Cromwell and many other English rulers, who had taken Ireland from the Irish people, tried to destroy the Church in Ireland. Every one of them failed. The hills of Ireland have been wet, again and again, with the blood of martyrs.

Today a free Ireland faces the Atlantic and the stars. Ireland has never deserted the faith of her fathers. The Irish have been true to God and God has been true to them. The memory of Patrick and the faith of Patrick have endured.

BAPTISM OF CLOVIS

WHEN we think of Europe today we think of such countries as France, Germany, Spain, Belgium, Holland, Switzerland, Portugal, Poland, Czechoslovakia, Yugoslavia, Romania etc. Each country is independent of every other country.

The map of Europe in the fifth century is different. We notice the absence of the names by which the modern countries of Europe are called. Europe was occupied by various wandering tribes and not by settled races.

The greater part of what is now France, was occupied by a Germanic tribe called the Franks. Besides the Salian Franks and the Tournai Franks and other branches of this Germanic tribe, there were Germanic tribes in France known as the Burgundians, the Alemanni, the Visigoths and many others.

Gaul was the Latin name for France. It was in Gaul that Julius Caesar became famous as a conqueror. Caesar's conquest of Gaul, however, was only a little thing when compared with the conquest of what is now modern France by Clovis (466-511 A.D.).

For thirty years, from 481 to 511 A.D., Clovis, King of the Salic Franks, fought to unite all the tribes in Gaul into a single nation. One by one he warred upon and defeated their rulers and secured their loyalty.

During one of his campaigns Clovis married a Catholic queen called Saint Clotilda. At that time Clovis was a pagan. In the midst of his battle against the Alemanni, we are told, Clovis had the same experience as Constantine the Great. The battle was going against him. His soldiers were weakening. The enemy were unmoved. Clovis saw his dream of a united nation disappear.

He thought of his beloved wife Clotilda. He knew she must be praying for him. Suddenly, Clovis was moved to pray to the Christian God of his wife for victory. Humbly he prayed that God would give him victory. His prayer was heard. Victory was won.

Like Constantine, Clovis began to study the Christian religion. Like Constantine, Clovis became a Christian. In the city of Reims, surrounded by three thousand of his soldiers, Clovis was baptized by Saint Remy.

Clovis chose Paris as his capital. The conversion and victories of Clovis made France a united and a Catholic kingdom.

Conversion of Central Europe

AS SOON as the Catholic Church was freed from the terrible persecutions of the pagan Roman Empire, bands of missionaries left Rome to convert the people of France and Spain and England and Ireland.

In Ireland the ancient pagan Druid priests disappeared. Before the end of the sixth century numerous large and active monasteries dotted the Irish landscape. Among the early leaders of Irish monastic life was Saint Finnian whose followers became known as the "twelve Apostles of Ireland."

It was in this seventh century that Ireland became the "Island of Saints and Scholars." The beams of her knowledge and her holiness shone out like a torch. The rest of Europe had been plunged into darkness by the barbarian invasions.

Out of the monasteries of Ireland and her sister country England came the monks who brought the message of Our Lord to the pagan tribes of Europe beyond the Rhine. Monks also came from the great Scottish Abbey of Iona, founded by the Irish missionary Saint Columba.

Through modern Belgium and Holland and Germany and Austria and Switzerland these monks from Ireland and England and Scotland labored for the cause of Christ. The waters of Lake Constance in Switzerland heard the voice of the Irish monk, Saint Columba. The name of Saint Gall is borne by a famous monastery in Switzerland.

Saint Wilfrid, the English monk, made the city of Utrecht, in modern Holland, his headquarters. Saint Winfrid, another English monk, traveled through the western part of Germany.

It was Pope Gregory II who changed the name of Winfrid to Boniface. The word "Boniface" means "to do good." Saint Boniface became the apostle of Germany. In 748 A.D. Saint Boniface was made Archbishop of the great city of Mainz. He was killed as a martyr by some German pagans.

Despite all differences of race and country the monks of the west united to spread the Kingdom of God. Thus it was that the Catholic Church united Europe in the Faith.

For a thousand years all European races were members of the Catholic Church. While they differed in many things, they were one in faith and hope and love. Not until the sixteenth century did they become permanently divided.

Rise of the Papal States

TODAY many good Catholics, when they die, leave something to their parish Church or to the Bishop in the diocese for works of religion and charity. From the very beginning the church has received such gifts of lands and buildings and money.

Catholic Kings of Europe once gave whole states or provinces as gifts to the Church. These large gifts of land were the real beginning of the Papal States. They were also called the Patrimony of Saint Peter.

In 754 A.D. a tribe of barbarians, known as the Lombards, left their home in northern Italy, and started for Rome, destroying all towns and farms in their path. Pope Stephen II appealed for protection to the King of the Franks, and Pepin subsequently came to Italy with his army and defeated Aistulf, the leader of the Lombards.

After his victory, Pepin returned to the Pope the lands which Aistulf had stolen away from the Church. In addition, he gave the Pope large territories in the northern part of Italy which the Popes were henceforth obliged to govern and protect against the ravages of the barbarians.

In 787 A.D. Charlemagne bestowed more territory upon the Pope. In 1115 a famous Catholic woman, the Countess Matilda of Tuscany, left her lands to the Pope and the Church upon her death. The Papal States then stretched from northeast to southwest across the center of Italy.

Neither the Popes nor the Church asked for the Papal States. Long before Pepin or Charlemagne, the Church was busy building her schools and her charities and protecting the inhabitants of Italy against the barbarians. The government of the Church was always gladly accepted by the people.

The Papal States were not seized by the Church. Their possession made the Church an independent power, with her own resources, so that she could really be a Catholic or universal Church.

The revenue she received from the Papal States was used by the Church for the glory of God, for the salvation of souls and for the service of humanity. The practice of leaving lands to the Church for such purposes has continued to our own day. The possessions of the Church are always at the disposal of the poor.

Mohammed Against Christ

FOR a thousand years, from 700 to 1700 A.D., Mohammedanism was one of the greatest enemies of Our Lord and His Church. The false religion of Mohammedanism, which is also known as Islam, was founded by a man named Mohammed.

Mohammed was born in 570 A.D., in Mecca, a city of Arabia. In his early life he was a shepherd. Then he worked as a guide and escort to the caravans or groups of traders who traveled by means of camels from city to city across the the deserts of Arabia.

Mohammed was interested in religion. He learned something of the Jewish and Christian religions during his journeys. He already knew something of the pagan religion of his own people, the Arabians.

In 610 A.D. he decided to become a preacher. Twelve years later he was driven out of the city of Mecca. He took refuge in the city of Medina where the people received his preaching more kindly.

The flight of Mohammed is called the "Hegira" from the Arabic word for "flight." The Mohammedans use the year 622 as the beginning of their calendar.

Mohammed preached that there was only one God whose name, he said, was "Allah." He called himself the prophet of Allah, and wrote a Mohammedan Bible called the Koran.

He commanded his followers to conquer all nations and either kill or enslave or convert them. The name of Allah became known as the Prince of War. Our Lord and Savior Jesus Christ has always been the Prince of Peace.

Mohammedanism was a religion of the sword. Again and again the Catholic nations of Europe trembled when they heard that the troops of Mohammed were on the march. Within one hundred years after his death, the false religion of Mohammed had crossed over the Straits of Gibraltar into Spain and France. There it was defeated.

Other false religions were destroyed by Mohammedanism. Only the true religion of Our Lord, the Prince of Peace, was able to stop the advance of Mohammedanism.

We should be grateful to the Catholic people and rulers of long ago who saved Europe from the savage and sensual religion of Mohammed. Once again the Church of Our Lord had saved the world.

BATTLE OF TOURS

WE HONOR the name of George Washington in the United States because he saved us from the tyranny of England. The French nation honors the name of Marshal Foch, who was a Catholic, because he saved France in the World War.

In the same way all Europe should honor the name of Charles Martel. It was he who saved Europe from the savage invasion of the Moorish followers of Mohammed.

In 732 A.D., one hundred years after the death of Mohammed, the followers of Islam had conquered Northern Africa, crossed the Straits of Gibraltar and marched through Spain. They then set forth to conquer the land which is modern France.

Nothing seemed to be able to stop them. Wherever they had conquered, they had murdered or enslaved the native population. They did not believe in brotherly love. They hated Our Lord and His religion. They were determined to destroy the Church and Christian civilization. They believed in perpetual warfare. In times of peace they lived only for pleasure.

They could only be stopped on the field of battle. Charles Martel (688-741 A.D.) ruled over the kingdom of the Franks. He had won their love and confidence. They looked to him as their deliverer from the fury and savagery of the Mohammedans.

If the followers of Mohammed had conquered France, all Europe would have been doomed. All churches and schools would have been destroyed. Christians would have been crucified in Mohammedan fury.

In 732 A.D. Charles went forth to meet the Moors. He met them, coming from Spain, at the city of Tours. All day long the battle raged. On one side was the Cross, the symbol of salvation. On the other side was the Crescent, the symbol of Mohammedan cruelty and slavery.

In the end the Crescent fell to the ground. The Cross of Christ gleamed proudly in the setting sun. The Moors retreated back across the border into Spain. They never returned to France again. Europe was saved, and the wonderful civilization of the Middle Ages was thus made possible.

Charles was henceforth to be known as "Martel" which means "The Hammer" or "The Conqueror." The Battle of Tours is one of the most important battles in the history of the world.

The Iconoclasts

THE Catholic Church has always had pictures and images of Our Lord, His Blessed Mother, the Apostles, and the Saints upon the walls of her Churches.

It is strange to read about the Iconoclasts of the eighth and ninth centuries of Christianity. The word "Iconoclasm" comes from two Greek words. The first part is from a Greek word "*eikon*" which means "*image.*" The second part is from a Greek word "*klaein*" which means "*to break.*"

Iconoclasm, therefore, means the breaking of images. An Iconoclast is a person who believes that images should be broken or destroyed. This hatred of images first appeared in Constantinople, the capital city of the Eastern Roman Empire.

In the eighth century a certain Leo III (717-740 A.D.) was the ruler at Constantinople. Contrary to the teachings of the Catholic Church, Leo, although he was a Catholic, wished to destroy all images. In the year 725 Leo decreed that all images should be destroyed.

The people arose in revolt. They loved the images of Our Lord and His Mother and the Saints. They refused to destroy them. Pope Gregory II (715-731 A.D.) took their part. Leo was forbidden to destroy the images. Pope Gregory III called together a meeting of 93 Bishops. Catholics were forbidden to become Iconoclasts. By the year 843 this heresy, or false teaching, of Iconoclasm was defeated.

Many years later, in England, the Puritans were also Iconoclasts. They destroyed the pictures and images which they found in the Catholic Churches they attacked. They falsely claimed that the use of images was a sin against the first commandment which commands us to worship God alone.

We Catholics know how false it is to say that Catholics worship images. We do not worship images. We use images only to recall the faces and lives of those whom we love. We worship no one but God. We honor Our Blessed Mother and the Saints.

It is not wrong to keep a picture of our mother near our bedside. Therefore it is not wrong to place the pictures or statues of Our Lord and His Blessed Mother upon the walls of our churches or our homes.

The Iconoclasts were wrong. The Catholic Church has triumphed over Iconoclasm as it has over every other enemy.

Coronation of Charlemagne

ON CHRISTMAS day, in Rome, in the year 800 A.D., a wonderful event was taking place. The King of the Franks, by which name the French were known over a thousand years ago, was being crowned Emperor of western Europe before the altar of Saint Peter.

He had been in the city for many days. Pope Saint Leo III (795-816 A.D.) was his friend. He had come with his soldiers to rescue the Pope from his enemies and from those who would destroy Christianity.

He was a big man, in heart as well as in body. In 771 he had become King of all the Franks. To educate his people he had brought scholars from all over the world. They taught in the schools which Charlemagne had built for his people.

He was interested in more than war. Although a soldier, he loved the arts of peace. He encouraged his people to become successful farmers and great scholars and talented musicians. Most of all, he encouraged them to become devout Christians. He loved the Pope who represented Our Lord and Savior Jesus Christ upon this earth.

When, therefore, Pope Saint Leo III journeyed over the Alps to beg his help against the enemies of the people, Charlemagne, or "Charles the Great" came and restored peace to the Eternal City.

The coronation of Charlemagne by Pope Leo III on Christmas Day in the year 800, was the beginning of the Holy Roman Empire which lasted for over a thousand years. Constantine the Great had recognized the power of the Pope. The Pope was now recognizing the power of an Emperor.

As long as there was a chance that the Emperor in Constantinople might return, no attempt was made to proclaim an Emperor in the West. Since the departure of the Emperors to Constantinople the Popes had done their best to guide and lead the people.

The Popes did not wish to be civil as well as spiritual rulers of Italy forever. Their duty was to spread the Kingdom of God. Civil rulers should rule over the empire of men.

The time had come. The man had come. Charlemagne, king of the Franks, was rightly crowned Emperor of Rome.

CONVERSION OF THE SLAVS

TWO brothers, Saint Cyril (827-868) and Saint Methodius (826-885) were born in Thessalonica. They might have risen to high positions in the government of the Eastern Roman Empire at Constantinople. They preferred, however, to enter a monastery. After their ordination to the priesthood, they returned as preachers to Constantinople.

In the year 863 A.D. they were sent as missionaries among the Slavs. Many modern peoples, such as the Bohemians and Poles and Russians, belong to the Slavonic race. The Serbs and the Croats were members of a particular Slavonic race known as Moravians. Since the lands of the Moravians were very near Constantinople, it was to Moravia that Saints Cyril and Methodius gave their learning and their lives.

The two missionaries were perfectly acquainted with the language and with the customs of the Slavs. They wished the Slavs to use the Slavonic language in the celebration of the Mass and in other official ceremonies of the Church.

In order to settle the question both Saint Cyril and Saint Methodius returned to Rome and consulted with the Pope. Pope Adrian II consented. As an indication of his approval the Pope had Mass celebrated in the Slavonic language in the four great basilicas or churches of Rome.

Saint Cyril having died, Saint Methodius returned to Moravia alone. While in Rome, Saint Methodius had been made Archbishop of the Slavs. Despite continued opposition on the part of those who objected to the use of the Slavonic language, the efforts of Saint Methodius were crowned with complete success.

Both Saints Cyril and Methodius translated the Gospels into the Slavonic language. This is another proof of the fact that the Church always has urged the people to read the Bible in their own language.

The Slavonic alphabet, which was invented by Saint Cyril, is the basis of the Russian alphabet and all other Slavonic literature. The modern state of Czechoslovakia embraces part of the territory to which Saints Cyril and Methodius brought the light of faith.

In the history of the East these two saintly brothers played the same part as the great Saint Patrick in Ireland, the great Saint Augustine in England and the great Saint Boniface in Germany.

Conversion of the North

THE countries called Norway and Sweden hang, as it were, from the top of the world. Nearby, across the Baltic Sea, is Denmark. In the beginning these three countries were united. The people were called Northmen or Danes.

They were a proud people. Like the ancient Greeks they loved the sea. They set out to sea in small boats. They were brave and warlike, and for that reason they were called Vikings.

Up the small rivers of the Franks they went on their plundering expeditions. Some of them settled on the west coast of France in the present French province of Normandy.

By the year 1000, Canute the Great, (994-1035 A.D.) remained King of Denmark. Under the wise rule of Olaf Haroldsson the land of Norway became independent.

In 1017, Canute the Great also became King of England. He proved to be a good Catholic and a good King. He brought peace to England.

In 1066 William the Conqueror, a Duke of Normandy, defeated King Harold, the last of the Saxon kings in England, at the battle of Hastings, and so became King William I of England.

The Northmen sailed as far south as Italy. There they defended Pope Gregory VII (Hildebrand) against the tyranny of the German Emperor, Henry IV.

There were Danes, or Northmen, in England long before the coming of Canute the Great. It was Catholic missionaries from England and Normandy who first brought the faith to these people of the North.

The Anglo-Saxon Bishop Sigurd is called the apostle of Norway. The first ruler of an independent Norway, Olaf Haroldsson, became a Saint. He is the Patron Saint of Norway today.

The most famous of the missionaries to bring the faith to the Northmen was Saint Ansgar. Saint Ansgar was a Benedictine monk from the famous Abbey or Monastery of Corbie.

In 826 he was able to baptize the King of Denmark. From Denmark he went to Sweden. By the end of the tenth century the conversion of the Northmen was complete.

The people of Norway and Denmark and Sweden are among the most highly civilized people in Europe. They owe most of their civilization to the Catholic Church which converted them from paganism.

Freeing the Slaves

THE Catholic Church which Our Lord founded taught that all men are equal in the sight of God. She rebuked the Roman slaveholders for their cruelty to their slaves. She urged them again and again to free their slaves.

Gradually many Roman nobles listened to her teachings. Shortly after the Church herself was freed from the Catacombs, a certain wealthy Roman, now known as Saint Melania, liberated thousands of slaves.

In the Middle Ages slavery no longer existed in Christian countries. Working men were known as serfs. The word "serf" was a word of honor then and not a word of dishonor as it is used today.

No longer could the workingman be sold together with his family. No longer was he a dependent beggar. He had his own plot of land and his own personal possessions. He had a right to wages. He rested on every Sunday and on the numerous holidays which the Church had established for bodily rest as well as divine worship.

The Church also established certain religious orders to ransom slaves taken by the Turkish pirates in the Mediterranean. The "Trinitarians" were founded in 1189 A.D. by St. John of Matha and St. Felix Valois. The "Trinitarians" are known to have ransomed nearly a million slaves from their Turkish masters.

The Order of Our Lady of Ransom, founded in the thirteenth century by St. Peter Nolasco, likewise ransomed half a million slaves from the Turks. The same work was done by the followers of Saint Vincent de Paul. Wherever slavery appeared, there the Catholic Church likewise appeared to stop it.

What Abraham Lincoln did for the negro slaves in the United States, the Catholic Church had already done for white and negro and Indian slaves all over the world.

Wherever the Church was listened to she changed the lives of all men for the better. The slaves became serfs and the serfs in due time became fully free.

By the end of the Middle Ages (1500) even serfdom no longer existed in Catholic countries. All men in all Catholic countries were free. Serfdom and slavery returned to the world only after men refused to listen to the teachings of the Catholic Church.

The Catholic Church deserves to be known as the mother of human freedom.

TRUCE OF GOD

OUR Lord is often called the "Prince of Peace." In one of His last talks with His disciples Our Lord promised them the gift of peace.

"Peace I leave with you: my peace I give unto you; not as the world giveth, do I give unto you. Let not your heart be troubled: nor let it be afraid" (John 24: 27).

In every Mass the priest, who represents Our Lord, prays for peace.

The history of the world has been filled with wars. During the Catholic Ages of Faith, wars were not as horrible as they are today. More men have engaged in warfare between 1500 and 1938 than in the entire thousand years between 500 and 1500 A.D.

During the Ages of Faith the Church was not merely satisfied with prayers for peace. She tried to maintain the peace of the world in two ways. She established the "Peace of God" and the "Truce of God."

By the terms of the "Peace of God" all persons who had dedicated their lives to God and all consecrated places were protected from warfare.

The "Truce of God" was established by the Church in the eleventh century. Every form of war was forbidden from Wednesday evening until Monday morning of each week. In addition, there was to be no fighting during the entire seasons of Lent, Advent and Easter.

For a thousand years the Church was able to encourage and maintain the peace of the world. In her pulpits and in her confessionals she insisted that her members give up the practice of warfare. In the sixteenth century in Europe occurred a terrible Religious Revolution against the Church. Since that century the most destructive wars in the world have occurred.

The "Peace of God" and the "Truce of God" were far more successful in preserving and increasing peace, than the so called peace pacts between nations in the twentieth century.

The world was a happier and more peaceful world when the nations and individuals listened to the voice of the Catholic Church. The voice of the Catholic Church is the voice of Christ, the Prince of Peace. The world will have peace only when all men and women return to the true worship of Almighty God.

Age of Chivalry

TO BE a gentleman is to be something that everyone admires. It is to obey the laws of God and of man. It is to show courtesy and consideration towards everyone. A gentleman never takes advantage of the weak. One of the purposes of all Catholic education is to produce ladies and gentlemen.

Paganism did not produce gentlemen. In pagan Rome and Greece most men were treated as slaves. To work at any trade was looked upon as the badge of a slave. Even the learned teachers whom the wealthy families of Greece and Rome employed as tutors for their children were considered slaves. The qualities of patience and purity and mercy and kindness did not exist in pagan Rome.

It was the Catholic Church which insisted on gentleness and gentlemanliness in life. Our Lord and Savior preached: "Learn of me because I am meek and humble of heart." In His sermon on the Mount Our Lord said: "Blessed are the merciful for they shall obtain mercy." The Saints were models of gentleness and gentlemanliness.

The word used to describe gentlemanliness in the Middle Ages was chivalry. For many years after the death of Charlemagne in 814 Europe was the scene of constant warfare between rival tribes. The Church tried to advance the cause of peace. She tried to soften the manners of men.

The Christian Knight was to be true to God. He was to become a Christian soldier. He was to fight on the side of the weak and oppressed. He was to be courteous towards all women. He was to be generous and merciful towards his opponents.

The young man who would become a Knight had to pass through a period of training. At the end of his training the Knight knelt before the altar. In the presence of God, he promised to conduct himself as a gentleman.

For nineteen hundred years the Church has been preaching the ideals of Christian chivalry. Whenever men have lived up to them the world has been happy. Whenever men have neglected or violated them the world has been unhappy.

The Catholic Church has always taught "love of God" and "love of neighbor." These are the qualities of true chivalry.

The Guilds

THE Catholic Church has been the greatest organizer of labor unions in the history of the world. Under her direction the Guilds, or Unions, of the Middle Ages were founded as early as the eleventh century. They were real unions for the protection of the rights of the workers and their families.

The first Guilds were called Merchant Guilds. They were formed to protect the rights of merchants against the tyranny of certain rulers. Some of those who owned the land tried to collect excessive taxes from the merchants who traded in the towns located on their lands.

The merchants united themselves in Guilds and refused to pay the exorbitant taxes. Many times they were able to secure town charters from the owners of the land. Their Guild thus became the town's government. In this way towns or cities first began to secure home rule.

To protect themselves against the tyranny of some merchants, workers also organized in what are called Craft Guilds. A craft means a trade. Thus the Tailors' Guild consisted of all those who followed the craft of tailoring.

The purpose of these Craft Guilds was to protect the rights of workers. They were open to all. They forbade high prices for goods. They trained the apprentices, or beginners at the trade, to become masters. They saw to it that both the apprentices and the journeymen, who worked for the masters, were properly clothed and housed.

No one was allowed to profit at the expense of anyone else. All goods had to be sold in the open market, and at a just price. Usury, or the taking of exorbitant interest for loaned money, was strictly forbidden.

The Catholic Church is still the friend of Labor Unions. All workingmen know this. The destruction of the Economic Guilds or Unions at the close of the Middle Ages, by the enemies of the Church, was a great disaster.

Life in the Middle Ages was happier for the workingman than it is today. The non-Catholic American poet Lowell agreed to this:

"The cup of life was never so full to overflowing, for the greatest and the least, as in those days when guildhood was in flower."

The Crusades

PALESTINE at the eastern end of the Mediterranean has always been an interesting country. It was the Promised Land promised by God to Abraham. In Jerusalem the Temple was built by Solomon.

In the time of Our Lord, Palestine was broken up into Roman provinces. Pontius Pilate was governor of Judea. Herod was tetrarch, or ruler, of Galilee. Philip, the brother of Herod, was tetrarch of Iturea. Lysanias was tetrarch of Abilina. The Jews were allowed to practice their religion. They held their own religious courts. They were free to worship in their Temple. But the country belonged to Rome.

The word "crusade" comes from the Latin word for cross, which is "crux." The Crusaders wore a large cross of cloth on their uniforms. In the eleventh century (1070) a tribe of Turks known as the Seljuk Turks captured Jerusalem on their march towards the West. They were followers of Mohammed. They were enemies of Christianity. It was no longer safe for Christians to go to the Holy Land and visit the places where Our Lord lived and preached and died.

Pope Urban II appealed to the Christian people and rulers of Europe. A great meeting was held at the town of Clermont-Ferrand in France in the month of November 1095. "God Wills It—God Wills It" shouted the multitude. The first Crusade was on. Peter the Hermit continued the work the Pope had begun.

The first Crusade succeeded in capturing Jerusalem in 1099. For nearly fifty years afterwards the Christians remained in the states of Jerusalem, Tripoli, Antioch and Edessa.

In 1144 the fall of Edessa inspired Saint Bernard to preach the Second Crusade 1145-1147.

There were eight Crusades in all. Whenever the Turks grew strong they defeated the Christians in Palestine. A new Crusade had to go against them.

In the end the Christians were obliged to abandon Palestine. In 1187 Jerusalem was re-captured by the Turks. In 1291 the last Christian towns were taken again by the Turks.

There were so many things to be done at home in Europe that the Christian rulers did not give their full support to the Crusades. Moreover, the Turks were united, while Europe, just as today, was divided. In the end the Crusades were abandoned.

In 1453 the Turks conquered Constantinople. Christians were now forced to fight them in Europe. The dream of taking the Holy Land had to be postponed.

CANOSSA

THERE have been two Roman Empires. One was the pagan Roman Empire which persecuted the Church.

The other Roman Empire began with the coronation of the Frankish King Charlemagne by Pope Leo III on Christmas day in the year 800. The first Roman Empire was a pagan Empire. The second Roman Empire was a Christian Empire. That is why the second Roman Empire is called the Holy Roman Empire.

Certain Emperors insisted that they and they alone should choose men to be Bishops. This led to many abuses, and the quarrel of the Emperors with the Church is known in history as the "investiture quarrel." The selection of unworthy men against the wishes of the Church caused many scandals. For this the Kings or Emperors who selected unworthy men were to blame and not the Church.

In the eleventh century a great Pope tried to stop these scandals. Pope Gregory VII (1073-1085) was born in 1020 and became a Benedictine monk. He led a holy life. Because of his learning four Popes kept him in Rome and followed his advice. As a monk he was known as Hildebrand.

One of his first acts upon becoming Pope in 1076 was to prevent the Emperor Henry IV from interfering in the selection of Bishops. Henry IV refused to obey. Then the Pope excommunicated the Emperor, but the people and Kings of Germany agreed with the Pope. They threatened to revolt against their Emperor.

Henry IV came to Italy seeking the Pope's forgiveness. He found the Pope at the castle of Canossa. For three days the Emperor stood outside the castle clad in the dress of a penitent. Finally convinced of his sincerity, the Pope forgave him.

The repentance of Henry IV, however, was not sincere. He returned to Germany and began to oppose the Church all over again. Advancing on Rome, Henry IV forced Pope Gregory to flee to the Abbey of Monte Cassino. There he died.

His dying words were: "I have loved justice and hated iniquity; therefore I die in exile."

In 1122 the freedom for which Pope Saint Gregory VII fought was won. Henceforth the Church was to be free in the selection of her Bishops for Germany.

Constantinople vs. Rome

CONSTANTINOPLE is the present capital of Turkey. It is situated on the European side of the Strait of Bosphorus. When it was settled by the Greeks in the seventh century before Christ, they called it Byzantium.

In 330 A.D. the Emperor Constantine made it the capital of the Roman Empire. The city was then renamed in his honor.

The religious head of the Church in Constantinople was known as the Patriarch. In 1043 a proud and ambitious man became Patriarch. His name was Michael Caerularius. He envied the position and authority of the Pope in Rome.

To enhance his own power and glory he inflamed the minds of the people of Constantinople against the Pope. Although Constantinople and Rome possessed the same faith and the same Sacraments, there were certain minor differences in the way of saying Mass and in receiving Holy Communion.

These differences were only local customs. Michael Caerularius insisted that such differences were important.

In order to settle these difficulties, Pope Saint Leo IX sent a representative to Constantinople. Michael Caerularius would not listen to him. He had already deceived the people into supporting him.

This disagreement between Constantinople and Rome has continued up to the present day. Greek Catholics believe in all that we do. They go to Mass and receive the Sacraments.

Some, however, refuse to acknowledge the supreme authority of the Pope. This separation between the Greek Church and the Latin Church is known as a "Schism" or division.

The Greek Catholics who are separated by this schism from the Pope call themslves "Orthodox Catholics." There are, however, many Greek and other Eastern Catholics who are united to the Pope of Rome just as we are. They are known as "Uniats," that is, Catholics united with the Pope in Rome.

After securing power over the Church in Constantinople, in 1054, Caerularius tried to take control of the Emperor and civil government. Here, however, he failed. The Patriarch was exiled to an island in the Sea of Marmora, where he died in 1059.

The return of all "Schismatic" Catholics to Rome is one of the things for which our present Holy Father is constantly working.

SAINT THOMAS À BECKET

MANY times we read about troubles between the Church and the State. The State has been responsible for most of these troubles. Long ago, many rulers interfered with the freedom of the Church just as they do today in Mexico and in Russia.

In the twelfth century King Henry II of England tried to exert his authority over the Church. He refused to allow Bishops to leave England without his permission.

When the Bishop of a diocese died, Henry II wanted the donations of the people to go to him instead of to the Church. He also wanted to select his own friends as Bishops in England.

The Church could not consent to this. Her champion in England was Saint Thomas à Becket (1118-1170). King Henry II was surprised and angry when Thomas à Becket opposed him. He himself had first appointed Saint Thomas to be Chancellor of England. He was glad when Pope Alexander III had raised Saint Thomas to the position of Archbishop of Canterbury.

As Archbishop of Canterbury, Saint Thomas remained loyal to the King as an English citizen. He also remained loyal to the Pope and the Church as a Catholic. He determined to fight for the freedom of the Church.

King Henry then became his enemy. Saint Thomas was forced to flee to France. When King Henry seemed to repent Saint Thomas returned. He kept up his fight for the freedom of all Catholics. One day in a fit of anger the King cried out for someone "to rid me of this insolent priest."

Four followers of the King took him at his word. They rode to Canterbury and found Saint Thomas in his cathedral. There they slew him (1170).

The death of Saint Thomas brought peace to the Church. King Henry II repented of his crime. The tomb of St. Thomas at Canterbury became the focal point of Catholic pilgrimages until another English King, Henry VIII, put a stop to them.

Saint Thomas was martyred for his loyalty to God and the Church. Like every good Catholic, he had kept the command of Our Lord to "render to Caesar the things that are Caesar's and to God the things that are God's."

Richard the Lion-Hearted

For East is East and West is West
And never the twain shall meet,
Till earth and sky stand presently
In God's great Judgment Seat.

But there is neither East nor West
Border nor breed nor birth,
When two strong men stand face to face,
Though they come from the ends of the earth.

RUDYARD KIPLING

RICHARD THE LION-HEARTED, King of England and Christian Crusader, came out of the West. Saladin, ruler and leader of the Seljuk Turks, came out of the East.

In the year 1187 Saladin re-captured Jerusalem. He immediately changed all Christian churches into mosques. "Mosque" is the name applied to a temple where the Mohammedan god "Allah" is worshiped.

The fall of Jerusalem aroused the Christian nations of the West. Two great kings responded. One was Richard of England. The other was Philip Augustus of France. For two years their allied troops waged battle before the Mohammedan city of Acre in Syria.

For two years the army of Saladin inside the walls of Acre held out. Finally the Christians won.

From Acre Richard marched southward. The troops of Saladin followed him. At a place called Arsouf the two armies engaged in battle once more. The swift horses of the Turks darted in and around the Christian hosts. The followers of Richard were killed by the hundreds.

Only the bravery of Richard inspired them. He was here. He was there. His sword kept swinging like a pendulum through the air. "God and the Holy Sepulchre help us," he cried out!

For God and the Holy Sepulchre, Richard drove back the forces of Saladin. Once again the cities of Jaffa, Tripoli, Antioch and Tyre fell before the army of Richard. A meeting was arranged between Saladin of the East and Richard of the West. They exchanged gifts of friendship. They swore to keep their word. Henceforth, they agreed to live in peace.

Christians were to be permitted to make pilgrimages to the Holy Sepulchre in safety. Once again Mass was to be said in Jerusalem and in Bethlehem and in Nazareth. Richard the Lion-Hearted had conquered Saladin. The Third Crusade was a success.

46

Innocent III, Defender of the People

THE Holy See cannot leave persecuted women without defense; the dignity of king does not dispense you from your duties as a Christian."

These words were written in a letter sent by Pope Innocent III to Philip Augustus, King of France. The word "see" means the diocese of a bishop. The "Holy See" means the diocese of the Pope.

Philip Augustus had put aside his lawful wife, Queen Ingeborg. He tried to marry another. Divorce was forbidden by Our Lord and Savior Jesus Christ. Therefore it is forbidden by the Catholic Church. Pope Innocent III finally forced King Philip Augustus to obey the law of God.

In this letter Pope Innocent III shows that the Popes have always defended the rights of women. He also shows that both rulers and subjects must obey the laws of God and the laws of the Church.

In the time of Pope Innocent III some German rulers tried to become masters of the Italian people. The Pope sided with the people of Italy. He saved them from the tyranny of all foreign rulers.

In England, King John was interfering in the affairs of the Church and oppressing his people. Only the presence of the great Archbishop Stephen Langton prevented King John from becoming a tyrant.

The people of England, represented by their local rulers, called Barons, revolted against the tyranny of King John. The King was forced to sign a charter of English liberties at Runnymede, in June 1215.

This document is known as the "Magna Carta." All historians trace the beginning of English liberties to this "Great Charter." It was forced from the tyrannical King by his Catholic subjects. The King was prevented from becoming a royal dictator.

Whenever the common people were wronged by their rulers, Pope Innocent III defended them. Whenever Kings and rulers thought they could ignore the laws of God, Innocent III reproved and punished them.

In the time of Innocent III all Europe was Catholic. The people looked upon the Popes as their friends and protectors.

Pope Innocent III always worked for the rights of God and for the rights of humanity. He deserves to be known as the "Defender of the People."

Louis IX

THE thirteenth century, 1200-1299, has often been called the greatest of centuries. By the time it had opened the Church had civilized all the nations in Europe.

The kings and rulers of these nations were united under the spiritual guidance of the Pope. It was a time when Kings as well as peasants obeyed the laws of God and man. Some of the 13th century sovereigns lived such devout lives that they became Saints. We do not hear of many rulers becoming Saints in our day.

Such a King and such a Saint was Louis IX of France, 1215-1270. He became King at the age of eleven. He was fortunate in having, for his mother, the wise and saintly Blanche of Castile.

As a little boy he was taught to respect the rights of others, to be kind and merciful towards all and to realize that in the eyes of God he was no different from the rest of his people.

The power to rule which he had as King was not his own. It had come to him from God and he must use it for the welfare of all his people. Like everyone in France, he must obey the laws of God and he must be loyal to the Church which Our Lord and Savior had founded.

To be a good King, it was first necessary to be a good man. It was more important to be a good King and a good man than to be a great man and a great King.

These were the lessons which Louis, the boy-king, learned from the example set by his gentle Queen-mother Blanche.

For forty-four years Louis IX ruled over his people.

He made them loyal to God and to the Church by his example. He loved Our Lord and went forth with his army on two Crusades to rescue the Holy Land from the Turks.

He was with his army near the city of Tunis in Africa when he died. A good Catholic will always be a good citizen. A good Catholic ruler will always become a great ruler. We should pray to Saint Louis of France and ask him to pray for those who rule the world in which we live today.

THE "POVERELLO"

THE Italian word "poverello" means in English "the little poor man." This was the name by which one of the greatest Saints in the Catholic Church is known. Most people try to shun poverty. Saint Francis of Assisi (1182-1226) took the virtue of poverty as his bride.

In the midst of a war between the city of Assisi and the city of Perugia Saint Francis was taken prisoner. Upon his return to Assisi Saint Francis decided to give up the world.

His father was furious. He brought Francis before the Bishop of Assisi. There Francis returned to his father even the clothes which he wore.

His first work was to repair the little church of Saint Damian and the chapel of Our Lady of the Angels at Portiuncula.

One morning at Mass, in the year 1209, he heard the priest read the following words from the Gospel: "Do not possess gold nor silver, nor money in your purses: nor scrip for your journey, nor two coats, nor shoes, nor a staff."

Stirred by these words Saint Francis went out to live a life of poverty and of preaching. Many young men of the city followed him. The Franciscan Order was thus founded in the year 1209. It was finally recognized and approved by Pope Honorius fourteen years later.

Many women also wanted to live a life devoted to poverty and good deeds. Saint Francis chose a very holy woman, Saint Clare of Assisi, to have charge of these women. This congregation is known as the "*Poor Clares.*"

In order to help people living in the world to grow closer to God, Saint Francis also drew up a rule for them. This is the Third Order of Saint Francis.

In the year 1224 Our Lord rewarded Saint Francis by placing the marks of His own sufferings on the hands and feet and side of the Saint. This is what is known as the Stigmata of Saint Francis.

Saint Francis was beloved by all. Even the birds of the air and the beasts of the field listened to him and showed no fear at his approach.

By his poverty and preaching Saint Francis extended the Kingdom of God throughout the world. He was one of the greatest gifts ever given to the world by the Catholic Church.

Apostle of the Rosary

A RELIGIOUS community is a society of men or of women who have consecrated themselves to the worship of God and to the service of men.

Religious communities are sometimes called Religious Orders. Their members wear a special uniform or habit to show that they have left the world for God.

Thus the Jesuits, founded by Saint Ignatius Loyola, wear black. The Franciscans, founded by Saint Francis of Assisi, wear brown. The Dominicans, founded by Saint Dominic, wear white.

Saint Dominic was born in the province of Old Castile in Spain in the year 1170. He died in the city of Bologna, in Italy, in 1221. During the fifty years of his life Saint Dominic became a great scholar, a great teacher and a great defender of the Church.

When wicked men called Albigenses, from the city of Albi, tried to cause the people of southern France to revolt against the Church and against all government, Pope Innocent III called upon Saint Dominic for assistance.

Saint Dominic gathered together men who knew the truth and who were willing to go out through the country in order to teach the people the truth about God and the Church.

Thus in 1215 the Dominican Order of priests was established in the city of Toulouse.

Through prayer as well as preaching the efforts of Saint Dominic were crowned with success. In his fight with these wicked enemies of God and the people Saint Dominic made special use of the rosary.

This is the same rosary which we should say every day in order to protect us from harm and to unite our minds with Our Lord and His Blessed Mother. Preaching without prayer is powerless.

The prayerful preaching of Saint Dominic and his followers preserved the faith in southern France. A school for the teaching of girls was established in La Prouille at the foot of the Pyrenees mountains. The Church, as Saint Dominic shows, has always believed in the education of women.

At his death Saint Dominic left sixty houses of his Order behind him.

The followers of Saint Dominic are also known as the Order of Preachers. That is why they sign the letters "O.P." after their name.

Apostle of Learning

ACCORDING to the English poet Kipling a truly great man is one who can "walk with crowds and not lose his virtue or talk with kings and not lose the common touch."

Saint Thomas (1225-1274,) was such a man. He was related to two German Emperors, Frederick II and Henry VI.

In 1243, after studying at the monastery of Monte Cassino and at the University of Naples, he became a follower of Saint Dominic. At Paris he sat at the feet of the famous Dominican teacher, Saint Albert the Great. The rest of the class thought Thomas a bit stupid because of his size. Thomas, Saint Albert said, might look like an ox but in time the voice of this ox would be heard round the world. Having completed his study in Paris, Saint Thomas was summoned to Rome by Pope Urban IV.

After leaving Rome, Saint Thomas went to the city of Bologna. There, between the years 1265 and 1272, he wrote his most famous book, called the "*Summa Theologica*" or Summary of Theology.

Theology is the subject which tells us about God and God's relations with man and the world, both of which He created. This work of Saint Thomas contained everything that was known about God and man from the beginning of the world up to the thirteenth century.

Saint Thomas also wrote many beautiful hymns. Among them is the "*Adoro Te Devote,*" or "*Devoutly do I adore Thee,*" written in honor of the Blessed Sacrament. One of the prayers recited by every priest in his thanksgiving after Mass was also written by Saint Thomas.

Saint Thomas, despite his great learning, always preached simple sermons which the people loved to hear. Even in his great work his language was clear and concise. Unlike many modern writers he did not try to confuse his readers with big words and roundabout expressions.

He died on his way to a Church Council at Lyons in the year 1274. His teachings have received the official approval of every Pope. Pope Leo XIII made him the patron or guide of all Catholic schools and scholars.

Because of his holy life and holy writings he is often called the "Angel of the Schools."

Catholic Schools

"THE school follows the Cross."

Next to many Catholic churches we see a school. In this Catholic school there is a crucifix on the wall of every classroom. The day opens and closes with prayer. Some or all of the teachers are Nuns or Brothers. The Parish priests make it a practice to visit the school regularly.

Here Catholic boys and girls are taught all the subjects that are on the curricula of the Public or State schools. In addition, they are taught religion and are trained to love God and their neighbor.

Catholics have always built schools. When Saint Augustine went to England, he built schools as well as Churches. When Saint Boniface went to Germany, he built schools there. It was the Catholic Church that began the first school system in the world.

Besides schools for beginners the Catholic Church built schools for advanced learning—universities, for scholars and lawyers and doctors. Some of the greatest universities in Europe and America today were founded by the Catholic Church.

Popes and Bishops spent everything they had to bring learning to Europe and to train learned men in universities. At least one hundred and nineteen universities and thousands of parochial schools and high schools were founded by the Catholic Church in Europe alone.

In American History we read that Harvard University was founded in 1636; Yale University in 1701; Princeton in 1746; and Columbia University in 1754. The oldest University in America, however, was founded by the Catholic Church in Peru, South America, in 1557, only sixty-five years after Columbus discovered America. The oldest universities in Europe, such as the Universities of Paris and Bologna and Oxford were founded by the Catholic Church over five hundred years ago.

The Catholic Church was forced to rebuild her schools many times. Very often wars and persecutions destroyed them, but when the persecutions ended the Catholic Church immediately started to rebuild them all over again.

Our Lord said: "Going, therefore, teach ye all nations." Through her schools and universities the Catholic Church has obeyed Our Lord's command.

The right to teach is one of the powers which Our Lord gave His Church when He established her. The Church has produced scholars as well as Saints.

GOThIC CAThEORALS

NO ONE knows the names of those who built the Cathedrals of Europe. Sometimes it took several generations to erect these glorious memorials to man's spirituality. Aisle by aisle and column by column they were built in honor of God.

Through their beautiful stained glass windows the sun keeps shining as though God Himself were blessing them. Statues of the Saints stand around the wall in the presence of the Blessed Sacrament, just as the Saints themselves stand in the presence of God.

Flying buttresses or columns of stone add strength to the outside walls. Lovely spires point like fingers of prayer towards the sky.

Gargoyles or grotesque figures of men and demons and beasts serve as water spouts. Before their terrifying faces all evil spirits were supposed by the builders to halt and leave God's dwelling place alone.

These Cathedrals should really be called Catholic Cathedrals instead of Gothic Cathedrals. The name "Gothic" was applied to them by those who disliked the Church. The word "Gothic" comes from the "Goths," one of the many barbarian tribes which overthrew the ancient Roman Empire. The Cathedrals were not built by the Goths. They were not built until centuries after the Gothic invasion of Europe.

At first, in the eleventh century, the Church built her Cathedrals in the old Roman or Romanesque fashion. Christianity, however, was a religion of joy and hope and happiness. Their thick walls, round arches and their lack of windows made the Romanesque Cathedrals too heavy and too dark.

Romanesque Cathedrals were followed by Catholic Cathedrals. The round arch was changed to the pointed arch. Higher walls, broken by many stained glass windows, enclosed the worshipers of God.

By the twelfth century this form of Catholic art had become famous throughout Europe. Gothic or Catholic Cathedrals, built by the Bishops and unknown workmen of the Middle Ages, lay like jewels on the hills and plains of Europe.

Nothing more beautiful has ever been built. In the language of a poet, these Cathedrals are truly "frozen music."

These Gothic or Catholic Cathedrals show that the Catholic Church is the mother of beauty as well as the mother of truth. God is beauty. Nothing is too beautiful for the worship of God.

Giants of Music

FROM the beginning the Popes and Bishops and priests and monks of the Catholic Church have encouraged the art of music in every possible way.

The one hundred and fifty Psalms of the Old Testament were set to music by the Catholic Church. In every temple built by the Church the organ loft was a necessary part. The choir-masters and organists of the great European Cathedrals were the greatest musicians of their time. Special schools of music were established everywhere throughout Europe.

Pope Saint Gregory the Great (590-604) has become famous for the reforms which he brought about in the manner of singing Church music. Gregorian chant is the name given to a form of music which the Church uses in her own sacred services. In 1922 the Pope ordered all Bishops to have this Gregorian Chant used in Catholic services.

Over the radio some night you will hear a musical work produced by the famous Franz Haydn. Haydn (1732-1809) was a singer in the Catholic Church of St. Stephen in Vienna. He wrote many Masses. These are musical compositions which use the words of the Mass and which were written to be sung at Mass. He also wrote 125 symphonies. He never wrote anything without placing upon it the words: "Laus Deo." This means "Praise be to God."

There is Ludwig van Beethoven (1770-1827) whose *Mass in D* and whose nine symphonies are among the loveliest in the world.

There is Mozart (1756-1791) and Liszt (1811-1886) and Donizetti (1797-1848).

There is Franz Schubert (1797-1828) who wrote 500 songs. Schubert's *"Ave Maria,"* composed in honor of Our Blessed Lady, is the best known song throughout the world.

There is Cesar Franck (1822-1890). He wrote a beautiful hymn to the words *"Panis Angelicas"* (Bread of Heaven) in honor of the Blessed Sacrament. This hymn rivals Schubert's *"Ave Maria"* in popularity.

There is also Giuseppe Verdi (1813-1901) whose Operas are beloved in the United States and who is only one of the many Catholic writers of Operas.

Many other names could be mentioned. The music and songs of the Catholic Church are amongst the richest treasures of civilization.

Giants of Art

THE birth of Our Lord at Bethlehem was accompanied by the beautiful songs of the angels. The Resurrection of Our Lord at Easter took place in a beautiful garden.

The Church is the mother of beauty. Art is the expression of the beautiful in stone or color or form or sound. For nineteen centuries the Church has always been the mother of the arts. The greatest pictures hanging upon the walls of the world's museums are the portraits of Our Lord or the pictures of His Blessed Mother, called "Madonnas."

Catholic art was especially beautiful and prolific during the period from the thirteenth to the sixteenth centuries. Too many people remember only the Religious Revolution of the sixteenth century. Too many forget the names of Raphael and Michelangelo and Leonardo da Vinci. No other painters or sculptors have ever surpassed them.

It is rare to meet a man who is a master sculptor, architect, painter and engineer all in one. This, however, was the distinction of Leonardo da Vinci (1452-1519). His painting of the *Last Supper* has been copied thousands of times in every country throughout the world.

The *Sistine Madonna* of the painter Raphael (1483-1520), is but one of the many beautiful paintings of Our Lady that adorn the world.

As sculptor, painter and architect, Michelangelo has never known an equal. His statue of Moses and his decorations on the ceiling and walls of the Sistine Chapel in the Vatican sweep the heart of every visitor heavenwards.

Historians have used the word "Renaissance" or rebirth to indicate that period in which the Catholic Church produced her greatest art.

The names of Giotto, who died in 1337, and Fra Angelico (1387-1485), and Fra Lippo Lippi and Botticelli and Van Eyck and Bramante and Titian and Rubens and Murillo and Millet and Valesquez, together with scores of other painters, from every country and of every race, must be added to complete the picture.

Pagan art is cold and lifeless. Catholic art is warm and full of life. Catholic art has remained to charm the world and to breathe of the beauties of the life hereafter.

God is beauty as well as truth. His Church makes life beautiful as well as useful.

Giants in Literature

In THE time of Our Lord everyone could speak and understand Greek. That is why the New Testament was written in Greek. Only the well-educated knew Latin as well as Greek. Later on, Latin became the language of the common people.

Many centuries later such languages as French, Italian, Spanish and Portuguese developed from the Latin. Modern English developed from the German of the Angles and Saxons who settled in England.

It was Catholic priests and monks who first taught and spread the use of these European languages. Catholic authors were the first to employ them. Most of the greatest French and Spanish and Italian and Portuguese and German and English writers have been Catholics.

William Shakespeare the greatest English author is said to have been a Catholic. A Catholic named Geoffrey Chaucer, who died in 1345, wrote a book called "*Canterbury Tales*." He was almost the first to write in the English language.

Dante (1265-1321), who wrote a wonderful poem called the "*Divine Comedy*" was a Catholic. Petrarch (1304-1374), a poet who wrote over three hundred sonnets and many other beautiful poems, was also a Catholic.

In Spain, Miguel de Cervantes Saavedra (1547-1616), wrote many interesting and humorous tales about a character called "*Don Quixote*." Cervantes was a Catholic. Lope De Vega (1562-1635), the greatest writer of Spanish plays, was also a Catholic.

In France many great figures in French literature such as Moliere (1622-1673) were Catholics.

Cardinal Newman was a great Catholic English writer of the nineteenth century. All Catholics should know the works of the Catholic poet Francis Thompson (1859-1907).

The names of G. K. Chesterton, Hilaire Belloc, Paul Claudel, Sigrid Undset, Francois Mauriac, Alfred Noyes and many others too numerous to mention, taken from every country in Europe, are the names of Catholics.

We should be proud, then, that we are Catholics. Catholic writers have produced most of the world's greatest literature.

We Catholics love beauty and goodness as well as truth. Our religion is beautiful. That is why Catholics have written such beautiful books. That is why the literature written by Catholics is one of the world's greatest treasures.

The Babylonian Captivity

O N THE banks of the river Rhone in southern France lies the town of Avignon. Here for seventy years the Kings of France kept several Popes of Rome in captivity. In remembrance of the seventy years of exile which the Jews spent in ancient Baby- onia, this period of Church history is known as the Babylonian Captivity.

Many times during the Middle Ages (500-1500 A.D.), the Popes saved Europe from dire disaster. The people were protected by the Popes against the tyranny of Kings. Many wars between nations were prevented. Wicked Kings were forced to mend their ways.

The Catholic Ages of Faith were the most glorious of all the ages in which the world has existed. Men were probably happier than at any other time in the history of the world.

The Babylonian Captivity of the Papacy, then, was no fault of the Popes. A powerful King of France, Philip the Fair, had attempted to steal the possessions of the Church by excessive taxation. He also tried to appoint his friends as French Bishops so that he could make the Church his slave in France.

Pope Boniface VIII (1294-1303) declared that Philip the Fair, as a Catholic, was subject to the Church. The Pope urged the clergy of France to be loyal to their country and to support the King with money. But Pope Boniface VIII was determined that the Church in France would not become the slave of Philip the Fair.

Upon the death of Boniface VIII Philip waited until a Frenchman became Pope in the person of Clement V (1305-1314). In 1309 the Papal Court was then removed to Avignon where it remained for nearly seventy years.

Both Italy and Germany resented the control which the French Kings tried to exercise over the Popes in Avignon. Aided by the grace of God the Popes remained true to their character as fathers of all Christendom.

Finally in the year 1377, Pope Gregory XI (1370-1378) was able to return to Rome. There the Popes have lived until the present day.

The prayers of Saint Catherine of Sienna, who went to Avignon to plead for Gregory's return, were answered. The Babylonian Captivity was over.

Saint Joan of Arc

FOR many hundreds of years the kingdoms of England and France were always in a state of war. When William of Normandy became King of England at the Battle of Hastings, he did not give up the land of Normandy which he owned in France. The French rulers and people resented the presence of the English. Again and again they fought to unite their country.

In the fifteenth century the French King, Charles VII, was again at war with the English. In battle after battle the French had been defeated.

At this time when the lilies of France were being trampled by the English invaders, there was born in the year 1412 in the town of Domremy a little peasant girl named Joan d'Arc. Out in the fields with her flocks she used to think about the unhappy state of her country. She prayed that God would bless her King and permit him to be crowned in the old royal city of Reims.

At the age of thirteen she heard strange voices and saw strange visions. She had always been devoted to Saint Michael. She loved Saint Margaret and Saint Catherine. She saw them very clearly, as she sat in the fields, and she heard their message. It was God's will that she should go to the King and help him.

Joan laid aside her little peasant dress and donned the uniform of a soldier. At the head of the troops she marched to the city of Orleans which was surrounded by the English. In the battle that followed the English were defeated. The city of Orleans was free. In the same year, 1429, her earthly King, Charles VII, was crowned at Reims. One day while fighting with her troops at the city of Compiegne she was captured, and immediately handed over to the English.

The English, smarting under their defeat at the hands of a girl, were anxious to put her to death. They falsely accused her of being disloyal to the Church and to the Pope. She was tried and condemned to death unjustly before an ecclesiastical tribunal, as a heretic and a witch.

One morning in the year 1431 a great fire was lit at Rouen in France. The nineteen-year-old Joan was lashed to a stake. A furnace of flames roared about her gentle body. With the name of "Jesus" on her lips Saint Joan of Arc entered the court of the King of Kings in heaven.

Invention of Printing

IN OUR high schools and colleges we read the writings of Caesar and Cicero and Virgil in Latin. We also read the poems of Homer and the great plays of Sophocles and Aeschylus in Greek. These works were written long ago.

We also read today the sacred pages of the Holy Bible. The Old Testament was written long before the time of Our Lord. The Gospels and Epistles and the other books of the New Testament were written shortly after Our Lord's death and resurrection. Who preserved the Bible and the classics for all mankind?

Day after day, for centuries, the monks of Catholic Europe sat in their monasteries making copies or manuscripts of the Bible and of the literature of Rome and Greece. The word manuscript means "written by hand." The monks wrote by hand, first on parchment and later on paper. It was tedious work and it was hard work. For nearly fifteen hundred years this slow, painstaking, copying of the precious manuscripts continued.

With the invention of printing man received one of his greatest gifts. We owe the invention of printing in Europe to a Catholic named Johann Gutenberg.

Gutenberg was born in the German city of Mainz in 1400 and died there in 1467. By using movable type or letters on which ink could be spread, Gutenberg made it possible to produce thousands of copies for every one that could be done by hand. The first printed book in Europe was the Bible.

The invention of printing made possible the growth and rapid spread of the Church all over the world. By means of the printing press the Catholic Church increased the number of Bibles in use. She also printed thousands of copies of the great Latin and Greek classics.

The Catholic Church has welcomed every invention of science. She warns her children only against false scientists. Real science and true inventions bring us closer to God. It is God who has made all laws and it is God who has created all things. Science aids in finding them.

The true scientist is a man of God. The Catholic Church, which was founded by God, is also the friend of science.

The Vatican Basilica

THE word "Basilica" comes from a Greek word meaning "royal." It is used to describe the first buildings which served as temples of worship in the Catholic Church.

Basilicas were originally pagan temples. They were rectangular in shape. At one end of the Basilica the altar stood in a circular space known as the *Apse*. At the opposite end was a porch, called the *Narthex*. Those who were preparing to become Catholics were not admitted beyond the Narthex. The central space, from floor to ceiling was known as the *Nave*.

There are four beautiful and important Basilicas in Rome. They are the Basilicas of Saint Peter, of Saint Paul, of Saint John Lateran and of Saint Mary Major.

The Basilica of Saint Peter is also known as the Vatican Basilica. The word Vatican refers to all the buildings grouped around the dwelling place of the Pope.

The original church or Basilica of Saint Peter was built on the site of the circus grounds of the Emperor Nero. In the fourth century Constantine the Great replaced the original church of Saint Peter with a magnificent Basilica.

Twelve centuries later this Basilica started to decay. Pope Julius II summoned the world famous architect Bramante to rebuild it. The work was begun in 1450 and finished in 1626. The great dome that gleams against the blue Italian sky is the magnificent contribution of Michelangelo.

In the center of the Basilica lies the tomb of Saint Peter. There the great of the world have come to kneel in prayer. Besides the principal altar there are thirty-three other altars erected over the graves of Saints and Apostles.

To see the Basilica of Saint Peter's by day, is to see one of the modern wonders of the world. To see the Basilica at night, with its dome bathed in a glow of light and the stars gleaming down upon the columns of Bernini (1598-1680) that surround the piazza, is to catch a vision of heaven.

The Vatican Basilica of Saint Peter's is the nearest approach in stone and color to the visions of heaven which we read of in the Apocalypse.

Moors Expelled from Spain

THE Gospel of Our Lord was brought very early to the Spanish Peninsula. During his exile in Rome, Saint Paul traveled as far as Spain.

In every one of the ten official Roman persecutions, Spanish men and women laid down their lives for Christ. From the very beginning of Christianity Spain had become a Catholic nation.

In the fourth century the Visigoths captured Spain from Rome. Their inter-marriage with the native Roman population produced the Spanish people of today.

In the beginning of the eighth century King Roderic was ruler of Spain. Among his followers was a traitor, named Count Julian. Count Julian invited the Mohammedans in Africa to cross the Strait of Gibraltar (named after the Moslem general who was to undertake the invasion) and to take up their residence in Spain. In 711 King Roderic was defeated in the battle of Xeres de la Frontera.

For over seven hundred and fifty years the Moors tried to destroy every bit of the Christian civilization which they found in Spain. The followers of Mohammed hated Christianity. Churches were destroyed. The Crescent of Allah replaced the Cross of Christ.

The Mohammedans forced the Christians to work for them. With few exceptions, all Christian Churches were turned into Mohammedan mosques. The Mohammedans taxed the Christians into slavery. They murdered Christians by the thousands. At the entrance of every Moorish city Christians were crucified side by side with dogs.

Bit by bit great Spanish leaders in the north recaptured parts of Spain from the Moorish tyrants. Weakened by their wickedness the Moors were pushed nearer and nearer to the sea. In 1491 Ferdinand of Aragon and Isabella of Spain drove the last Moorish tyrants across the Strait of Gibraltar.

Spain once more was free. The Cross had conquered the Crescent. Civilization was restored in Spain.

Historians who do not like the Catholic Church are fond of writing about the glories of Moorish civilization in Spain. True historians know that the seven centuries of Moorish occupation were centuries of bloodshed and tyranny and slavery.

Spain was free before the Moors conquered King Roderic in 711. Spain was not completely free again until the Moors were expelled in 1491 by Ferdinand and Isabella.

Discovery of America

FIVE hundred years ago many people believed that the earth was flat. Many Catholic scientists believed that the earth was round. Christopher Columbus was one of them. By sailing westward across the Atlantic he hoped to reach the eastern shores of Asia.

Today, when we cross the Atlantic, we do so in big ships that have swimming pools, tennis courts, comfortable rooms and the best of food. It was, however, with only three small sailing ships, the Santa Maria, the Pinta and the Nina, and with only 120 men, that Columbus set forth from Palos on August 3, 1492.

Storms tossed the little vessels about like chips. For days at a time they rested upon the bosom of an unknown sea, waiting for a breath of wind to blow them on their journey. The food ran out. The water became bad.

The crew threatened mutiny. Again and again they begged Columbus to turn back. And again and again, the great Catholic Admiral replied: "Sail on."

We owe the voyages and discoveries of Columbus to Queen Isabella of Castile. The Franciscan Father, Juan Perez had persuaded her to support the Genoan admiral, when everyone else laughed at him. Columbus was only attempting to find a short trade route to the East; he did not dream of finding a new continent.

On the morning of October 12, 1492 his voyage was over. Not the mainland of Asia but one of the Bahama Islands appeared upon the horizon. Grateful to God, Christopher Columbus knelt upon the sand and erected the cross of Christ. In memory of Our Savior, Columbus called the island San Salvador.

A greater continent than Asia had been reached. A greater deed than the discovery of a mere trade route had been accomplished.

In 1493, in 1498 and again in 1502 Columbus returned to explore the islands of the Caribbean Sea and the mainland of South America. On his second voyage Father Juan Perez accompanied him. The first Mass in the new world was said on the island of Haiti.

Two Catholic rulers, one Catholic priest and a great Catholic admiral, who trusted in the sea and in God who had made the sea, accomplished the discovery of America.

Westward ho!

AFTER the discovery of the New World by Christopher Columbus other nations of Europe sent out men to explore it. Most of the explorers of North and South America during the sixteenth century were Catholics.

Every European nation was anxious to own territory in America. Thus the English settled in New England and Canada. The French settled in Canada and in the Mississippi River Valley. The Portuguese settled in modern Brazil. The Spanish, the greatest explorers of all, settled in Central America, in the West Indies, in South America and in the southeast and southwest of the United States.

The colonial claims of England were based on the voyage of John and Henry Cabot. The Cabot brothers were Italian mariners in the service of King Henry VII of England. They, too, were Catholics.

The colonial claims of France were based on the voyages of Verrazano, of Cartier, of Champlain and many others. They were all Catholics.

The colonial claims of Spain were based on the voyages of Columbus and on the explorations of De Soto, Cortez, Pizarro, Balboa, Ponce De Leon, and many others. They were all Catholics.

The name "America," which was given to the new continent, was taken from the name of Amerigo Vespucci. Amerigo Vespucci was an Italian mariner in the service of the King of Portugal.

In the Hall of Fame at Washington, there is a large statue of the great Jesuit missionary, Father Marquette. In 1673 Father Marquette and Louis Joliet, another Catholic, traveled in small boats down the Mississippi. They were the first white men to explore the "Father of Waters." In 1682 another French Catholic, La Salle, after great hardship reached the mouth of the Mississippi where New Orleans now is located.

The first names of lakes and rivers and cities in America were Catholic names. Thus the oldest city in the United States is Saint Augustine in Florida. Lake George was once known as the Lake of the Blessed Sacrament. The city of San Francisco (Saint Francis) recalls the Spanish Franciscans who civilized the western coast of our country.

Catholics should be proud of the part played by their ancestors in opening up the new continent of America to the world. The science of exploration was a Catholic science.

Apostles of Freedom

UNFRIENDLY historians are fond of repeating that the Spanish explorers came to Mexico for gold. They do not tell their readers that during the sixteenth century many other nations of Europe came to America also for the sake of gold. The Spaniards were not the only ones.

The Spaniards came to this country also for the sake of religion. It was in this spirit that Ferdinand and Isabella wrote about the first voyage of Columbus: "He is bound for certain parts of the ocean to transact business of interest both to God and to us."

Priests accompanied all the Spanish explorations. While the Spanish explorers in Mexico and Central and South America and the United States investigated the new continent, the priests labored among the Indian population. The savage Indians were taught the truths of Christianity and civilization. The Church always fought to protect the natives from cruelty.

Thus, through the efforts of the Jesuits in Paraguay, the Indians were housed together in villages called "reductions." The civil rulers disliked this because it took the native population out of their control.

The Jesuits defended the Indians against any attempt to enslave them. They also taught the Indians how to cultivate the soil and how to build houses. They were taught to become carpenters and masons and blacksmiths and printers. The Jesuits persuaded the Indians to use only a part of their crops. The rest was stored in warehouses for future use.

Even Voltaire, an enemy of the Church, publicly praised the work of the Jesuits among the Indians in Paraguay. He referred to the "reductions" as "the triumph of humanity."

It was a Dominican Bishop, Bartolome de las Casas, who journeyed to Spain in order to free the Mexican Indians from slavery. The saintly Bishop was successful. The Indians were settled in villages of their own. Only one third of the Indians were permitted to work in the mines and then for only two months of the year.

Through the efforts of the Catholic Church slavery was abolished in Mexico in 1537. This was three hundred years before slavery was abolished in the British Empire and in the United States.

COUNCIL OF TRENT

WE MUST always remember that the Catholic Church is human as well as divine. The members of the Church are men and women. Popes and Bishops and priests are also men. All who belong to the Church and all who govern the Church are commanded to be good and holy.

From time to time, unfortunately, throughout the history of Catholicism a few leaders of the Church have followed in the footsteps of Judas, instead of in the footsteps of Saint Peter or Saint John the Beloved. They themselves are to blame. Those who do wrong should be blamed rather than the Church to which they belong.

And yet, this is exactly what certain men tried to do in Europe in the sixteenth century. Martin Luther in Germany and Ulrich Zwingli in Switzerland and John Calvin in France and John Knox in Scotland all did their best to destroy the Catholic Church on the pretense that their doctrines were intended to reform the membership of the Church.

These men did not reform anyone. Martin Luther was an Augustinian priest and monk before he defied the Church. Later in life, he was sorry for his disobedience. He called the Protestant Reformation a failure.

"If I had to begin all over again," he said, "I would leave the great masses of the people under the direction of the Pope; for these people are not amending their ways with the Gospel, and are only abusing the freedom that has been granted them."

In the sixteenth and seventeenth centuries the Pope Paul III called together the nineteenth General or Ecumenical Council. This Council was called in the city of Trent in Austria on December 13, 1545. There the Pope and Bishops stated once again the great truths which Our Lord had left to His Church. There they passed laws against all the sins of which certain members of the Church were guilty. There they also ordered the publication of a catechism, "The Catechism of the Council of Trent."

The Protestant Reformation was a failure. It only succeeded in making the lives of the people worse. It was a revolution and not a reformation.

The only reformation was that produced by the Catholic Council of Trent, 1545-1663. Loyalty to the Church means loyalty to God.

THE SOCIETY OF JESUS

ONE day a Spanish soldier in the army of Ferdinand and Isabella of Spain lay wounded at Pampeluna, the capital of Navarre, which had been attacked by the French. He was unable to return to battle. He had many hours to think about his life. Many times he had risked his life for his King, but he had done very little in the service of Christ, the King of Kings.

Reading a translation of Ludolphus' "Life of Christ," the young soldier's heart became inflamed with love of Our Lord. As soon as he was well, he renounced the world, and determined to live for Our Lord alone. This Spanish soldier was Saint Ignatius of Loyola (1491-1556) the founder of the Society of Jesus.

Ignatius left the world. He retired first to the great Benedictine abbey of Montserrat and then to Manresa to pray and to grow close to God. There he wrote his famous *Spiritual Exercises.*

Ignatius next went to Paris in order to study. There he became a learned man. There, also, he met Saint Francis Xavier and several others. In 1534 they became the first members of his religious community.

Ignatius and his companions offered their services to the Pope. In 1540 Pope Paul III approved their society and their work. Not until much later, and then only by those who disliked them, were the members of the Society of Jesus called Jesuits.

The foundation of the Society of Jesus is one of the most important events in the history of the Church. In the sixteenth century false leaders were drawing many Catholics away from the Church. The Protestant Religious Revolution had just begun.

Ignatius and his Society of Jesus rallied to the defense of the Church. The Society devoted itself to education: education of the mind and of the soul.

Within one hundred years the Society of Jesus had spread all over the world. Jesuit schools and colleges were established in every country in Europe. Jesuit missionary priests brought the message of Our Lord to America and to Asia.

By their example and by their numerous schools the Jesuits saved whole nations for the Church. The forces of the Protestant Revolt were defeated.

In 1622 Ignatius the soldier became Ignatius the Saint. He had lived and died in the service of the King of Kings.

The Great Reformer

SOME unfair historians are always fond of praising those who deserted the Catholic Church. They are not so fond of praising those who remained true to the Church of Our Lord, or of those who became converted to the Faith.

In the sixteenth century God raised up several wonderful men to save the Church from the attacks of her enemies. Saint Charles of Borromeo (1538- 1584) was one of them. He became Archbishop of Milan over a thousand years after the same honor had been conferred upon Saint Ambrose.

After studying at the University of Pavia he was summoned to Rome by his uncle Pope Pius IV. He was only a young man, but the Pope placed him in control of all lands belonging to the Church. The people, especially the citizens of the Papal States, were pleased with the appointment.

Saint Charles, however, was more interested in saving his soul than in earthly glory. In the year 1564 he retired to Milan. There he spent the next twenty years of his life serving God and serving his beloved people.

During the year 1576 a terrible plague descended upon the city of Milan. Many people left the city in order to avoid the disease. Saint Charles remained. He turned his own house into a hospital. He nursed the sick with his own hands. He held the dying in his arms. He had no fear for himself. He did what every good priest and Bishop of the Catholic Church has always done.

To instruct his people he founded the Confraternity of Christian Doctrine. Through this Confraternity he trained over five thousand teachers to instruct the poor in the truths of Our Lord.

He was only forty-six when he died. The plague had spared him, but his daily labors in the cause of Our Lord had worn him out. His holiness, his charity and his kindness made everyone love him.

The life of Saint Charles Borromeo may be said to have recompensed the period for the wicked lives of those who attacked the Church. The Church should be praised for Saint Charles Borromeo and for the many other Saints and holy men whom she has trained.

At the news of his death Pope Gregory XIII said: "A light has been extinguished in Israel."

Battle of Lepanto

IN 1453 the Turks after many attempts finally captured the ancient city of Constantinople.

In 1571 the Moslems prepared to follow up their victory by massing a huge fleet in the Gulf of Lepanto ready to strike at the Christian League of Nations. Europe itself was divided by the Protestant Revolution. The Turks thought that the time had come for the final destruction of Christianity.

Our Lord and Saviour, Jesus Christ, however, was still present in His Church, just as He had promised to be. Some rulers of Europe displeased Him by their unchristian life and conduct. But there were other rulers who loved Christ and His Church. They were anxious to protect her.

Thus it was that the great Catholic king, Philip II of Spain, the Venetian Republic, and Emperor Charles V answered the call of Pope Pius V. A Christian fleet supplied by Venice, Spain and the Papal States under the leadership of the great Don Juan of Austria, son of Charles V, sailed to meet the Turkish fleet.

As the Turkish fleet on that October day of the year 1571 rounded the headlands in the Gulf of Lepanto, off the shores of Greece, the Turk, Ali Pasha, never suspected what was in store for him.

A smile appeared upon his lips as he took up his binoculars to see what was ahead. Suddenly his smile vanished. He shouted commands in the Arabic language. His soldiers leaped up from the decks where they were resting. They rushed to the side of the vessel. Not victory, but a Christian fleet, under the command of Don Juan of Austria was ahead. In short order Ali Pasha's galley was captured and panic had spread to the Turkish squadrons.

The Turkish fleet was destroyed. The bodies of 25,000 Turkish soldiers sank beneath the waves. Planks on the surface of the sea showed where Turkish vessels had disappeared under the brilliant and gallant attack of the Christians. Some 15,000 Christians in the Moslem galleys were liberated.

Europe was divided, but the Christian fleet was united. They were fighting for God and His Church and for the civilization of Europe. The Christians knew no fear. They would have been glad to die. But they lived to sink the Turkish fleet in the Straits of Lepanto.

The Battle of Lepanto was decisive. Never again would any Turkish fleet set forth to destroy Christianity and civilization in the Mediterranean.

The Gregorian Calendar

IN ALL Catholic countries a strange thing happened in October, 1582. The people went to bed on October 4th and woke up on October 15th! This was done in order to make the calendar accurate.

A calendar is supposed to show the number of days which are required for the earth to move around the sun. For many centuries it was thought that the earth took 365 days to go round the sun. In the time of Julius Caesar this number of days was found to be inaccurate. Thereupon, Julius Caesar established the Julian Calendar. He added an extra day every fourth year in the month of February. The year with the extra day is known as a Leap Year.

In the time of Pope Gregory XIII (1572-1585) it was discovered that the earth went around the sun in a little less than 365 and ¼ days. This meant that since the time of Julius Caesar the earth was ten days further around the sun than the calendar showed.

To have our calendar correct it was necessary to recover the ten days which had been lost. Pope Gregory XIII consulted with Catholic scientists. He then ordered that October 4, 1582 should be followed by October 15, 1582. With few exceptions every fourth year was to remain a Leap Year. Pope Gregory XIII thus arranged to keep our calendar scientific and accurate. Taking his name, our calendar since that time has been known as the Gregorian Calendar.

Scientists everywhere admitted the truth of the Pope's findings. The sixteenth century, however, was the time of religious revolution. Countries which wickedly broke away from the Catholic Church refused to follow the Pope, even though his scientific findings were correct.

England did not adopt the Gregorian Calendar until 1752. The Russians and the Greeks refused to make their calendars accurate until the time of the World War.

We should be proud that our present calendar begins with the birth of Our Lord. We should also be proud that the Catholic Church always has been interested in science.

Real science is truth and all truth comes from God. Pope Gregory XIII is only one of the many Popes who encouraged the study and teaching of science.

The English Revolt

WHEN, in the 16th century Martin Luther wickedly attacked the Pope and the Church of Our Lord, Henry VIII, King of England (1509-1547) rose to the defense of the Church. As a reward Pope Leo X bestowed upon Henry the title of "Defender of the Faith."

The time came, however, when Henry VIII wanted Pope Clement VII to divorce him from Catherine of Aragon, his lawful wife. Henry then dreamed of marrying Anne Boleyn and making her his queen. Pope Clement VII refused to do so.

The English King then decided to ignore the Pope and to follow his own desires. Henry VIII made Parliament pass what is known as the Act of Supremacy which declared that he and not the Pope was the head of the Catholic Church in England.

The Tudor Monarch was able to intimidate his courtiers and most of his subjects. There were two, however, who were not afraid. One was the saintly Bishop John Fisher. The other was Saint Thomas More. Both were imprisoned in the Tower of London. Both suffered death because they remained faithful.

After the Act of Supremacy, Henry VIII then made Parliament pass the Oath of Succession in order to force people to admit that the marriage of Henry and Anne Boleyn was lawful. Next Henry VIII made Parliament pass the Treason Laws. Those who acknowledged the spiritual authority of the Pope were called traitors.

Henry VIII, to punish the monasteries which had remained faithful to the Church, ordered Thomas Cromwell to close them, to confiscate their possessions and distribute them among his followers.

Soon, even Anne Boleyn was beheaded by Henry's orders. In the years that followed Henry VIII had four other wives. Jane Seymour died at the birth of her son, Edward VI. Anne of Cleves was divorced because of her ugliness. Catherine Howard, like Anne Boleyn, was beheaded. Only Catherine Parr outlived the King.

Henry VIII also persecuted the Protestants who came to England from the continent. Catholics and Protestants, alike, were compelled to suffer as a result of his tyranny. Sin had darkened his mind and weakened his will.

When Henry VIII died, England was freed from a brutal tyrant who had murdered two wives, defied the Pope and abused his own people.

Tyranny of Elizabeth

THE first trouble between England and the Church occurred during the reign of King Henry VIII (1509-1547). But Henry did not introduce Protestantism into England. He passed laws against Protestants and Catholics alike.

On the death of Henry, Edward VI (1547-1553) the son of Jane Seymour, Henry's third wife, succeeded him. King Edward VI was only ten years old. He was controlled by his uncle and by those who wished England to become Protestant.

The laws of Henry against Protestantism were repealed. All Englishmen were obliged to worship God according to the rules of the Book of Common Prayer. The sacrifice of the Mass was forbidden. The Protestant Archbishop Cranmer of Canterbury destroyed all Catholic altars, vestments and ornaments.

Edward VI was succeeded by Queen Mary (1553-1558) the daughter of Henry VIII and Catherine of Aragon. Queen Mary was a Catholic. Naturally the friends of Henry VIII and Edward VI were displeased and fearful of their security. They were angered when Queen Mary condemned certain religious disturbers to death for treason.

At her death Queen Mary left the English throne to Elizabeth (1558-1603), extracting the promise from the daughter of Henry VIII and Anne Boleyn that she would defend the rights of the Catholic Church in England.

But Elizabeth immediately broke her promise. Once again all Englishmen were forced to use the Book of Common Prayer. All Catholic Bishops and priests were removed. All who insisted upon obeying the Pope in spiritual matters were branded and executed like traitors. Many Catholics, their property confiscated, fled to the continent in order to secure religious peace and religious freedom.

Queen Elizabeth was one of the most bigoted rulers who ever sat upon the English throne. She lacked the womanly qualities of mercy and tenderness. All the laws against the Catholic faith which have disgraced the history of England began then.

Unfair and prejudiced historians have tried to call Queen Mary of England "Bloody Mary." And yet Queen Mary sent only 284 leaders of the Protestant revolution to their death.

Queen Elizabeth murdered thousands of Catholics. Queen Elizabeth deserves the title "Bloody" before her name far more than Queen Mary.

Apostle of Charity

WHENEVER we see the name of Saint Vincent de Paul, we think of a Society which bears his name. A conference or branch of the Society of Saint Vincent de Paul is in nearly every Catholic parish.

It consists of a group of Catholic men who help the poor by their prayers, their visits, their advice, and their almsgiving. This society was established by the great Catholic Frenchman, Frederick Ozanam (1813-1853).

Why did Frederick Ozanam give the name of Saint Vincent to the society which he established in 1833 for the relief of the poor?

Saint Vincent was born in the year 1576. Twenty-four years later, in 1600, he was ordained a priest. His life was full of action. Once he was captured at sea by Mohammedan pirates. They bound him in chains and threw him into the hold of their vessel. When they reached Africa they sold him as a slave. After two years he succeeded in converting his master. Together they returned to France.

There, because of his learning and brilliance, Saint Vincent was invited to the homes of the rich and the powerful, but he elected to live his life among the poor.

In 1625 he gathered together a group or community of priests to go out and preach the Gospel among the poor. Saint Vincent's community was approved by the Pope, and became known as the "Congregation of the Missions." The followers of Saint Vincent are also known as "Vincentians."

In addition to their work of instructing and helping the poor, the priests of Saint Vincent established seminaries where men were trained for the priesthood.

With the help of Saint Louise de Marillac, Saint Vincent soon founded a religious community of women known as the Sisters of Charity. Before the end of the seventeenth century the spiritual sons and daughters of Saint Vincent had appeared everywhere.

The life and labors of Saint Vincent prove that the Church has always been the mother and helper of the poor.

The names of the Kings of France in the seventeenth century are almost forgotten. The name of Saint Vincent de Paul who died in 1660, is known and loved throughout the world.

American Martyrs

NEARLY three hundred years ago many Jesuit priests left their homes in France and sailed across the ocean to Canada in the New World to disembark at Montreal or Quebec. From there they traveled through the virgin forests of America. A thousand miles and more they marched and paddled their bateaux along the lakes and rivers through the interior of New France. They made their homes with the American Indians in New York State. They preached about Our Lord and His Church. They converted many Indians before they died.

Father Isaac Jogues and his fellow priests chose to work among the Huron Indians. The Iroquois Indians were enemies of the Hurons. In 1642 a small band of Iroquois seized Father Jogues and kept him a prisoner for twelve months.

In 1645 Father Jogues again returned to America from France. He was eager to stop the war between the Iroquois and the Hurons. At Auriesville, in the State of New York, Father Jogues met with the Iroquois chiefs, but they would not listen to him.

On his third missionary journey to America Father Jogues once again fell into the hands of the Iroquois at Lake George. He was tortured and slain.

One by one, his fellow Jesuits—Father Anthony Daniel, Father Charles Gamier, Father John de Brebeuf, Father Gabriel Lalemand, Noel Chabanel, Rene Goupil and John Lalande—followed him to a martyr's grave.

In 1654 the Iroquois Indians finally conquered the Hurons and practically exterminated them. The successors of Father Jogues tried to convert the savage Iroquois. This time their work was more successful.

The work of Father Jogues had not been entirely in vain. An Iroquois village was established near Montreal. There the saintly Indian girl, Catherine Tegakwitha lived and died.

The blood of the Jesuit Martyrs had watered the soil of the new world. The "Lily of the Mohawks," as Catherine Tegakwitha is called, was the harvest of their martyrdom.

On September 26th we celebrate the feast of these Jesuit martyrs. Father Jogues was the first priest to come to Manhattan Island which is now the City of New York. He was one of thousands who left their native land, with all its comforts, to labor for Our Lord in the wilderness.

Glorious Poland

THE Polish people have always been devout Catholics. Poland, like Ireland, has always suffered greatly for the faith. The sanctuary of Our Lady of Czenstochwa has become famous all over the world.

Poland's greatest tragedy occurred between the years, 1772 and 1795. Bit by bit her territory was taken away from her and divided between Austria, Russia and Prussia.

Foreign rulers persecuted the Polish people and their Church. The persecution was worst in that part of Poland stolen by Russia. Polish schools were closed. Polish children were forced to attend Russian schools. Lands belonging to the Catholic Church in Poland were taken forcibly by the Russian government.

Through this dark night of racial and religious persecution the Polish people remained true to their God, to their Church and to their country. One of the few good results of the World War was the reestablishment of Poland as a free nation in 1918.

The name of the Polish King John Sobieski (1629-1696) is the name of one of the greatest Catholic heroes in the world. In the year 1683 the Turks made one last attempt to force their way into central Europe. They had already taken over a great part of Hungary. Now their armies were knocking at the gates of Vienna. The whole Christian world appealed to John Sobieski to save them.

On the plains of Austria, like Richard the Lion-hearted, the Polish King rode everywhere across the field. He knew that he must conquer to save Europe for Our Lord. The Crescent must not be allowed to destroy the Cross.

At the news that John Sobieski was on the field, the Turkish army gave way. Mile by mile the Polish army pursued them. Never again did the Turks return to threaten Vienna and the Christian lands to the West. Civilization was saved from the menace in the East.

Like a true Catholic John Sobieski gave full credit for his victory to God. "I came," he wrote to Pope Innocent XI, "I saw, but God conquered."

The Christian world owes John Sobieski and the Polish nation an eternal debt of gratitude.

The glory of Poland, like the glory of Ireland and all other Christian nations, is the glory of the Catholic Church.

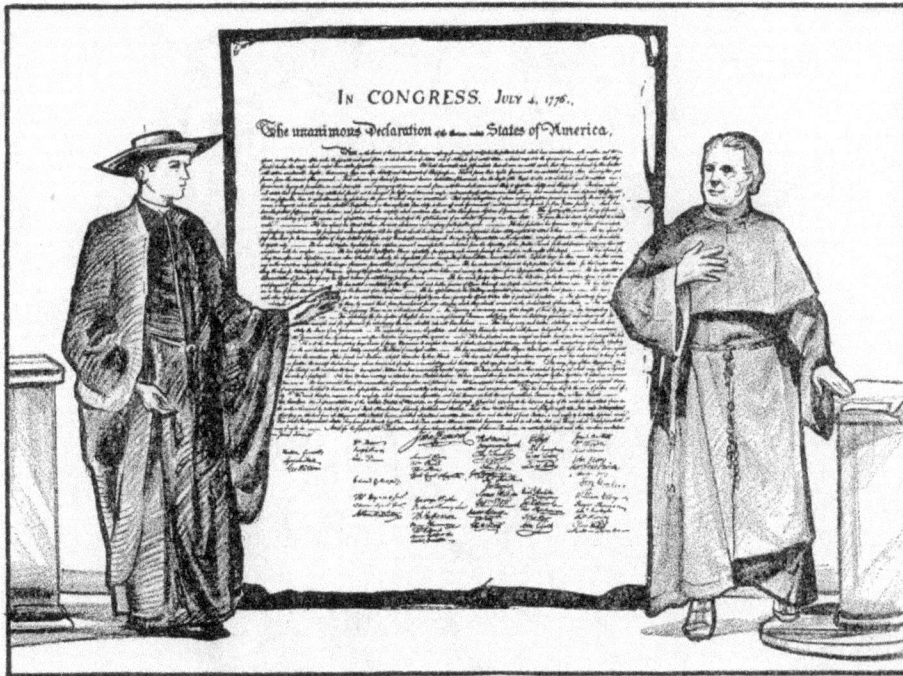

Democracy

ON JULY 4, 1776 the Continental Congress adopted the American Declaration of Independence. Thomas Jefferson was its author.

"We hold these truths to be self-evident, that all men are created equal, that they are endowed by their Creator with certain inalienable rights, that among these are life, liberty and the pursuit of happiness. That to secure these rights, governments are instituted among men, deriving their just powers from the consent of the governed."

This paragraph from the preamble of the Declaration contains the following truths of democratic government.

1. All authority comes from God.
2. God has created men with certain inalienable rights. This means that God has given every man and every family certain rights which no government should ever attempt to take away from them.
3. Just governments derive their right to govern from the consent of the governed.

Where did the founders of our American Democracy get these ideas? They did not make them up by themselves. They did not get them from the English government at the time of the founding of Jamestown (1607). For, at that time, the English Kings ruled like dictators.

These principles of democratic government came from the teachings of the Catholic Church. Some of them can be found in the writings of Saint Thomas Aquinas. All of them will be found in the writings and teachings of two great Jesuits, Robert Bellarmine (1542-1621) and Francisco Suarez (1548-1617).

The tyrannical Kings of England and other countries in Europe during the 17th and 18th centuries hated the democratic teachings of Saint Robert Bellarmine. His writings were destroyed in England.

The teachings of the Catholic Church on democracy were known to Thomas Jefferson, to James Madison and to other members of the Continental Congress. The book containing the democratic teachings of Saint Robert Bellarmine used by Thomas Jefferson can be found in the Library of Congress today.

The writings of Saint Thomas Aquinas, of Saint Robert Bellarmine and of Francisco Suarez, prove that the Church has been the mother of democracy.

Colonial Religious Freedom

IN THE seventeenth century many people were persecuted for their religion in Europe. Many came to America in order to find religious freedom.

In 1620 the Pilgrim Fathers, who were Puritans, landed at Plymouth to worship God in their own way. The Puritans in turn, however, did not give religious liberty to others. They drove Roger Williams into the forests of Rhode Island.

In 1634, Catholics, who were being persecuted by the English government, came to the colony of Maryland, founded by Cecil Calvert, the second Lord Baltimore.

A Jesuit priest, Father White, accompanied the first settlers to Maryland. The first settlement of Catholics there was at the village of Saint Mary's.

For many years the Catholic settlers of Calvert's colony lived peacefully side by side with their Protestant neighbors. Later, a bigoted man named Clayborne persecuted the Catholics and deprived them of their rights.

Lord Baltimore had given full freedom to the Maryland settlers to set up their own form of government. As a Catholic he had the right to expect that his own people would be tolerated and respected.

He appealed to the Assembly or governing body of Maryland for fair play.

As a result, in 1649, the first Act of religious freedom and toleration was passed in the United States. The Act referred to all those who believed in Christ. It did not mention other religions outside of Christianity, because there were no such religions in the Colony. This famous "Act Concerning Religion" declared that "no persons believing in Jesus Christ should be molested in respect to their religion or the exercise thereof, or compelled to adopt the belief or exercise of any other religion against their consent."

In 1683 Thomas Dongan the Catholic Governor of the province of New York persuaded the first Assembly of New York to pass "A Charter of Liberties" which guaranteed the right of religious freedom.

With the exception of Pennsylvania and Rhode Island no other colony tolerated religious freedom.

Never once in the history of the United States have Catholics or the Catholic Church been guilty of persecuting their fellow non-Catholic citizens.

Catholics have only the greatest love for all their non-Catholic neighbors.

The First American Bishop

IN THE winning of our independence from England Catholics played an important and successful part. There were many Catholics in the Colonial Army. Father Peter Gibault helped George Rogers Clark to secure the loyalty of all people in the Ohio Valley. Four prominent Catholics were among the signers of the Declaration of Independence. One of these was Charles Carroll of Carrollton. The other was Daniel Carroll, the brother of John Carroll (1735-1815). John Carroll became the first Bishop in the United States.

The life of Bishop Carroll is full of patriotism and divine romance. He was born in Maryland. In 1753 he entered the Society of Jesus. In 1769 he was ordained a Jesuit priest. In a short time the abilities and activities of Father Carroll made him the leading churchman in the colonies.

At the request of the Continental Congress, Father Carroll accompanied his relative Charles of Carrollton, Benjamin Franklin and Samuel Chase on an official mission to Canada. The Continental Congress wanted the Canadians to support the American Revolution.

The failure of this mission was not due to Father Carroll or his associates. It was due to the existence of religious bigotry in certain colonies. The people of Canada feared that they would lose their religious freedom if the Colonists won.

In 1789, the year of the adoption of the Constitution of the United States, Father Carroll became Bishop of all Catholics in the United States.

Under the wise guidance of Bishop Carroll the condition of the Catholic Church in the United States improved. The Sulpician Fathers, driven out of France by the French Revolution, were invited to Baltimore to start a seminary and a college. The year 1791 marks the beginning of the present University at Georgetown.

In 1808 Bishop Carroll became Archbishop of Baltimore. In the same year the dioceses of New York, Philadelphia, Boston and Bardstown (now Louisville) in Kentucky, were formed by Pope Pius VII.

Archbishop Carroll was beloved by all people, non-Catholic as well as Catholic. He saw the Church firmly established in the United States before he died.

The name of Bishop Carroll is entwined with the name of George Washington in the memory and love of every Catholic American.

CALIFORNIA MISSIONS

CALIFORNIA is a land of sunshine and of beauty. Along the road from San Diego to the north the evening air rings with the sound of mission bells.

The loveliest thing to be seen in California is not the Golden Gate and San Francisco Bay. It is not even the Sierra mountains whose crests are wreathed in snow and whose foothills are clothed with flowers and giant trees. What everyone remembers upon coming away from California are the California Missions.

These California Missions were more than churches. They were centers of civilization. Besides the church and rectory, each Mission contained a school, a shop and a workroom where the Indians learned the useful arts of industry, as well as a guest house where every traveler along the road from Mexico to San Francisco was welcomed.

No native of California can ever forget the history of the Franciscans and the name of Father Junipero Serra (1713-1784). He was born on the Island of Majorca. He was still a young man of twenty-seven when he joined the Franciscan Order. He was still young when, in 1749, he volunteered to go and preach among the Sierra Gorda Indians.

He was an old man, just beyond the three score years and ten, when he died. He has left us a few of his writings in the form of personal letters and official reports. His greatest deeds were written in stone and adobe across the State of California and on the hearts of the Indian tribes who loved him and who followed him.

In 1769 Father Junipero Serra built the first mission in what is the modern State of California at San Diego. Eight other mission centers of religion and education, of Christianity and civilization, were also left by him at intervals of a day's march apart along the road to the North.

In 1822 California became a part of Mexico. In 1834 the Mexican government dispossessed the Franciscan Friars of the Missions and turned them over to paid officials. As a result, the Indians were deprived of civilization and of employment. Many of them returned to war and paganism.

Today the Missions are historical records of the past. In Father Junipero Serra's day they were the only centers of civilization in the golden west. Around them lingers the memory of the holy Franciscans who gave their lives to the Indians for the cause of God

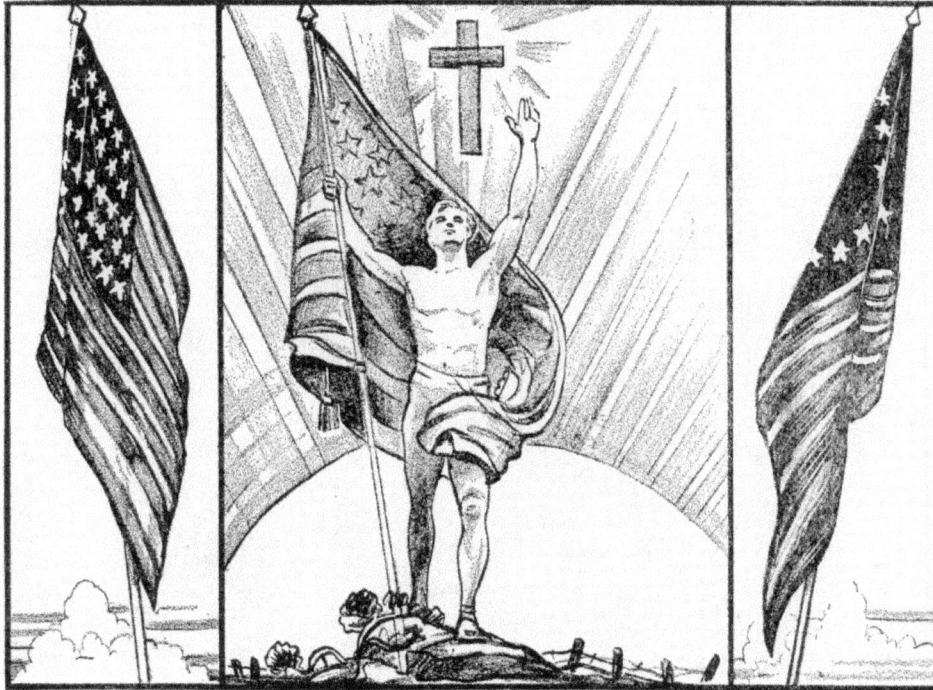

TWO GREAT WARS

W E CAN always be proud of the part played by Catholics in every age of our country's history. The first naval battle of the American Revolution was fought under the leadership of Captain John Barry, a Catholic. In 1794 George Washington founded our present American Navy. Commander Barry was placed at the head of it. He is known as the "Father of the American Navy."

From various lands in Europe Catholic military geniuses came to America and donated their services to the American colonists. The names of Lafayette, Steuben, Rochambeau, Kosciusko, DeKalb and Pulaski, who were Catholics, must never be forgotten in any history of the American Revolution. Without the aid of Catholic France the American Revolution would have been lost.

When the war was over George Washington wrote to all Catholics in the United States as follow:

"I presume your fellow-citizens will not forget the patriotic part you took in the accomplishment of their Revolution and the establishment of their Government, or the important assistance they received from a nation in which the Roman Catholic faith is professed."

Throughout the tragic days of the World War our nation knew that it could count on the fullest cooperation of all Catholic citizens. Father Duffy, chaplain of the famous Sixty-Ninth Regiment of New York, and Major General O'Ryan, commander of the famous Twenty-Seventh Division from the North, are Catholic names surrounded with glory. The highest ranking officer in the United States Navy was the Catholic Admiral Benson.

It was the brother of a Jesuit who finally led the forces of the Allies to victory. Marshal Foch, a devout Catholic, had stopped the victorious advance of the Germans toward Paris, in the Battle of the Marne. In 1918 Marshal Foch was placed in supreme command of all the Allied forces.

At the time of the World War, Catholics were only about 17% of the total population of the United States. And yet Catholics composed 35% of the army; 40% of the navy and 50% of the marine corps.

In peace and in war Catholics have always been loyal to the government of the United States. Their fellow-citizens should always remember it. Catholics will always defend their country against all her enemies.

Pius VII and Napoleon

THE mention of the name Napoleon awakens many memories. Napoleon was an Italian born on the island of Corsica, which at that time belonged to France. He became ruler and Emperor of the French. He tried to conquer the world. He failed.

He was forced to retreat from Moscow, where the biting winds of winter were sharper than the bullets of the enemy. He was finally defeated by the English and Prussians at Waterloo, in Belgium. He died a prisoner on the Island of Saint Helena.

Napoleon's greatest opponent, however, possessed no sword and led no army. He was Pope Pius VII, born in 1740; sixty years of age when he became Pope in 1800; and eighty-three years old when he died in 1823.

In 1806 the struggle between Napoleon and Pius VII began. The Emperor desired the Pope to annul the marriage which his brother Jerome Bonaparte had contracted with Miss Patterson, an American girl from Baltimore. To annul a marriage means to declare that the marriage never took place. Pius VII refused. Napoleon became furious.

Since he was at war with Russia and England, Napoleon wanted the Pope to exile all English and Russian people who were living in the Papal States. This, too, the Pope refused. Thereupon, Napoleon seized the Papal States for himself.

The Emperor then decided to select his own friends as Bishops in France. The Pope excommunicated him. Napoleon retaliated by seizing the Pope and keeping him a prisoner at Fontainebleau.

Meanwhile, the enemies of Napoleon were gathering new armies against him. The Pope was sent back to Italy in 1814. Napoleon was obliged to give back the Papal States to the Pope. One year later Napoleon was defeated at Waterloo.

Many broken dreams crossed the mind of Napoleon as he waited for death on the island of Saint Helena. He asked Pope Pius VII for the services of a chaplain. The Pope granted his request.

Attended by this chaplain the Emperor of France and the Dictator of the world passed before the judgment seat of God.

All good Catholics must live for God. This life is very brief. Even the greatest Emperor must leave it all too soon.

Catholic Emancipation Act

FOR almost three hundred years, every English ruler, from Queen Elizabeth to King George III, tried his best to destroy the Catholic religion in England and Ireland. The English persecution of Catholics and the Catholic Church continued until a little more than one hundred years ago.

To be a Catholic priest was to be guilty of treason. The teaching of the Catholic religion was forbidden. The property of Catholic children who went abroad to study was confiscated by the English government. Catholics were ordered to attend Protestant services. When they refused to do so, they were fined. When they continued to refuse they were outlawed.

No Catholic, of course, was allowed to vote or to become a member of Parliament. All members of the English and Irish Parliament were obliged to denounce the Holy Eucharist, the Mass and the Catholic practice of honoring the Saints.

Irish Catholics were not allowed to own or to lease property. The English government rewarded anyone who spied upon the Irish Catholics and reported their attendance at Mass.

In time, however, sincere and fairminded Englishmen like Edmund Burke and Henry Grattan revolted at this English persecution of Catholics. Not until 1771 were Catholics in Ireland permitted to lease land. Not until 1792 did Catholics receive the right to vote.

The Catholic population of England and Ireland then found a stalwart leader. He was a great Irish Catholic. His name was Daniel O'Connell. Despite British threats Catholics used their votes to elect Daniel O'Connell from County Clare to Parliament. He refused to take the British Oath against his religion. Despite his election the British Parliament closed its doors upon him. Again he ran, and again he was elected. The people were aroused. In the end King George IV and his parliament surrendered.

On April 13, 1829, the Catholic Emancipation Bill was passed. Daniel O'Connell took his seat in Parliament amidst wild applause and rejoicing.

Catholics were admitted to all public offices except a very few. No member of Parliament was forced any longer to take an oath against the Catholic Church.

Three hundred years of persecution were over. Daniel O'Connell long will be remembered as the savior of his people and the defender of his Church.

The Oxford Movement

Lead, kindly Light, amid th' encircling gloom
 Lead Thou me on;
The night is dark, and I am far from home,
 Lead Thou me on.
Keep Thou my feet; I do not ask to see
 The distant scene; one step enough for me.

THIS is the first stanza of one of the loveliest poems in the English language. It was written by John Henry Newman (1801-1890), before he became a Catholic.

He was looking for truth and light just as the captain of a ship looks anxiously through the fog or the storm in order to find a safe harbor.

John Henry Newman was an Anglican or a member of the Episcopal Church of England. He was a brilliant scholar, an eloquent preacher and a great writer. He became a teacher at Oriel College of Oxford University which had been founded by Catholics around the year 1180. Later, Newman became Vicar of St. Mary's Church which was attended by the teachers and students of Oxford University.

Nobody in the United States could conceive of the President as the head of any Church. Yet, in England, all who belonged to the Anglican Church looked upon the King of England as the head of their Church. The English Parliament made all of the laws for the Church.

Newman objected to this. In 1833, with a group of other members of his church, Newman started to write pamphlets or tracts against government interference. He and his followers protested when the English government appointed, as English Bishops, men who did not believe in all the tenets held by the Anglican Church.

This protestation by Newman and his associates is called the Oxford Movement and is not to be confused with the present Oxford movement of the Buchmanites. The studies of Newman gradually led him to a knowledge of the Catholic Church. This Church alone, he discovered, went back to the teachings of Christ. Catholics have remained true to Christ's principles. The Catholic Church still maintains all the Sacraments and the truths Christ taught.

There was only one thing to do. In 1845 Newman resigned as Vicar of Saint Mary's. He became a Catholic. Later he became a priest. In 1879 Pope Leo XIII made him a Cardinal. The "Kindly Light" of faith had led him to the harbor of Saint Peter.

Nineteenth Century Revival

FROM the sixteenth to the nineteenth century the Catholic Church experienced unremitting and cruel persecutions in many countries. Penal laws were passed against her in England and Ireland and Germany and France. Her schools were closed. Her priests and bishops were killed. Her members were deprived of their property and of their freedom.

Unfair historians have even tried to lead people into forgetting the wonderful things accomplished by the Church during the centuries of Catholic civilization. These centuries, from 500-1500, have been called by Ralph Adams Cram, a distinguished Episcopalian architect, "the great thousand years." Our Lord who suffered death on Calvary for our salvation, rose from the dead on Easter Sunday. So, the Catholic Church has always risen to great heights of glory after every persecution.

In the nineteenth century, however, we find thousands of people in every country turning to the Catholic Church. In France a great Catholic named Chateaubriand wrote that "Christianity is the most practical, the most human, the most favorable to freedom, arts and letters."

The great French Dominican, Lacordaire, attracted thousands by his beautiful and truthful sermons. In 1833 Abbe Migne founded the Catholic newspaper, called "*L'Univers*" (The Universe).

In Germany, Leopold von Stolberg and Princess Galitizin, who was the mother of a famous American missionary priest, spoke and wrote about the glories of the Catholic Church. By studying the history of the Catholic Church Joseph von Gorres became a Catholic and the founder of the first Catholic newspaper in Germany called "*Katholik.*"

In the middle of the nineteenth century a German Jew, named Karl Marx, tried to arouse all people against their governments. Even today the writings of Karl Marx are used to stir up revolution. But it was Bishop von Kettler of Mainz who showed the world that the Catholic Church, and not Karl Marx, was the friend of the poor and the oppressed.

After three hundred years of modern persecution, the Catholic Church has once again appeared triumphant. Her scholars and her Saints have filled the world with praise.

Once again she appears as the friend of the poor and the light of the world, even as Our Lord had destined her to be.

Councils of Baltimore

UP TO the year 1784 all Catholic priests and people in the United States were governed by religious superiors in England. In that year the Rev. John Carroll was appointed by the Pope as Prefect Apostolic or ruler of all Catholics in the country.

Five years later he became a Bishop. In 1793 the first student to become a priest in the United States was ordained in Baltimore.

Within the past one hundred and fifty years the Catholic Church has grown to a degree never dreamed of by the early priests who labored in Baltimore under the direction of Bishop Carroll. One hundred and fifty years ago there were only 15,000 Catholics in Maryland, 7,000 in Pennsylvania, 1500 in New York and 200 in Virginia. Today there are over twenty million Catholics in the entire United States.

Much of the growth and development of the Church in the United States is due to three great gatherings of the Bishops held in Baltimore. These meetings are known as the three Plenary or General Councils of Baltimore. One was held in 1852. The second was held in 1866. The third was held in 1889.

In the First Plenary Council of Baltimore (1852) plans were laid for the establishment of a parochial school system of education. A Catholic school was to be built in every parish. Today we have the finest parochial school system of education in the world. A Catholic student can secure a complete system of Catholic education, from the first grade of a Catholic elementary school to the last year of graduate study in a Catholic university.

In the Third Council of Baltimore arrangements were made for the publication of the Baltimore Catechism. This text book of Christian doctrine is used in all our parochial schools.

The names of three great churchmen in Baltimore— Bishop Carroll and Archbishop Kenrick and Cardinal Gibbons—will always be associated with the growth of our country as well as of our Church. They were patriots as well as churchmen. They were loved by non-Catholics as well as by Catholics.

In Baltimore, the Church as we know it today had its beginning. There, too, under the early Catholic settlers, was the birthplace of religious liberty in America.

Archbishop Hughes

SAINT PATRICK'S CATHEDRAL is known throughout the United States. It is the most beautiful Gothic structure in the western world. Its cornerstone was laid, in 1858, by Archbishop Hughes.

Archbishop John Hughes was born in Ireland in 1797. He was ordained in Philadelphia in 1826. In 1842 he became Bishop of New York. In 1851 Pope Pius IX raised him to the rank of an Archbishop. He died in New York in 1864. He loved the city and the people among whom he worked.

Catholic education in the United States is one of the Church's brightest jewels. Archbishop Hughes founded the parochial school system in New York. He also built a seminary for the training of priests.

About this time certain people who called themselves Native Americans and "Know-Nothings" tried to deprive all Catholic citizens of their rights as Americans. They were prejudiced and bigoted. They did their best to harm the Church. As a Catholic and an American Archbishop, Hughes fought against them and defeated them.

Real Americans must love their neighbors. They must permit all citizens to worship God in peace.

The "Know-Nothings" and Native Americans were enemies of religious freedom, and that is why they failed as political parties and are all but forgotten.

When the Continental Congress desired the help of Catholics in the American Revolution, Archbishop Carroll of Baltimore was glad to help.

So, too, when President Lincoln and the United States Congress requested the aid of Archbishop Hughes in the midst of the Civil War, they found him ready and willing and anxious to serve. He did not allow the memory of the Catholic persecutions by the "Know-Nothings" and Native Americans to deter him. He knew that the American government was not responsible for them, for they were not truly Americans.

In 1861, at the request of the government, Archbishop Hughes went to France in order to secure the loyalty of the French for the cause of the Union in the Civil War. The United States has always been grateful for his leadership and diplomacy.

Midway between the time of Archbishop Carroll and the time of Cardinal Gibbons stands Archbishop Hughes. Like them, he was loyal to God, loyal to Church and loyal to his country.

English Catholic Revival

THREE great Cardinals were the leaders of the Catholic Church in England during the last half of the nineteenth century. One was Nicholas Patrick Wiseman (1802-1895). The other was John Henry Newman (1801-1890), a convert. The third was Henry Edward Manning (1808-1892), likewise a convert.

For nearly two hundred and fifty years the Catholic Church had no Bishops or dioceses in England. The work of the Church was carried on by certain priests known as Vicars Apostolic, appointed by the Pope to assume control over church affairs.

In 1850 the Church decided to restore her Bishops and Archbishops to England. Nicholas Wiseman, who had been a priest and a teacher in Rome for twenty years, was made Archbishop of Westminster. He was also created a Cardinal. England was likewise divided into a number of Catholic dioceses with a Bishop at the head of each.

This action on the part of the Church aroused a storm of bigotry throughout England. There were anti-Catholic demonstrations and mass meetings. Newspapers, including the *Times*, denounced the Pope. Even John Russell, the Prime Minister, protested.

Encouraged by the government and the press, mobs burned figures of the Pope and Cardinal.

A less learned and prudent man than Cardinal Wiseman might have ruined the day. While protesting with dignity against this outbreak of religious bigotry, the Cardinal waited while the storm grew less violent and gradually disappeared.

In the midst of the agitation William Henry Manning became a Catholic and a priest. At the death of Cardinal Wiseman, Cardinal Manning became his successor. By the time of Cardinal Manning's death all England had forgotten the disturbances which greeted the return of the Catholic Hierarchy to England.

The English people remembered with gratitude how Cardinal Manning had settled the London Dock strike and his ardent love for the poor.

Our Lord said: "Blessed are the meek, for they shall possess the land." The meekness of Cardinals Newman, Wiseman and Manning, as much as their learning, restored the power and glory of the Catholic Church in England.

English Catholics are among the most loyal sons and daughters of the Church.

The Roman Question

IN THE nineteenth century many attempts were made by armed enemies of the Church to take away her temporal power, Papal States in Italy. At that time Italy was not a united nation. Italy consisted of many independent kingdoms. There was no King of Italy.

In the year 1848, Pope Pius IX was asked to become the head of a united Italy. Violent enemies of the Pope however invaded Rome. They killed Count Rossi, one of the Pope's representatives, on the lands of the Church. Pope Pius IX was obliged to flee for his life to the kingdom of Naples.

The Pope appealed for protection to his Catholic subjects in Europe. Troops from France and Spain and Austria and Naples restored the Pope to Rome. A small number of French soldiers were stationed in Rome in order to protect the Pope against future violence.

In 1860 the troops of a revolutionary named Garibaldi tried once again to seize the Papal States. In 1870 Napoleon III, Emperor of the French, withdrew the French soldiers from Rome.

The troops of Victor Emmanuel, who was King of Piedmont, invaded the Papal States. Pius IX refused to engage in bloodshed, but he protested against this violation of the rights of the Church.

On September 20, 1870 the city of Rome was seized. Victor Emmanuel proclaimed himself King of Italy.

Pope Pius IX became a voluntary prisoner in the Vatican. He refused to leave the Vatican until the Italian government repented. This is the beginning of the "Roman Question."

In May, 1871 the Italian government passed what is known as the "Law of Guarantees." According to this law the Church was to receive over a half a million dollars a year to make up for the lands that had been taken away from her.

Pope Pius IX refused to accept it. He also refused to become a subject of the King of Italy. If the head of the Church is to remain free, the Pope cannot be subject to any earthly power.

Since 1870 all Italy has been united under one King. Not until Pope Pius XI settled the Roman Question by the Lateran Treaty in February, 1929, did any Pope feel free to leave the Vatican.

The Vatican Council

THE year 1870 was a year of great tragedy and also of great triumph in the history of the Catholic Church. It was in this year that the last possessions of the Popes in Italy were taken away by the Italian government. It was also the year in which the doctrine of Papal Infallibility was solemnly declared before the whole Christian world.

On December 8, 1869 Pope Pius IX opened the sessions of what is known as the twentieth Ecumenical Council of the Catholic Church. The Vatican Council lasted until October 20,1870. It was attended by Bishops from all over the world.

Our Lord promised that the Spirit of Truth would always be with His Church to protect her from error. He said that He would remain with her all days "even until the consummation of the world." When Our Lord promised to make Peter the head of the Church he also promised that "the gates of hell would not prevail against her."

According to the teachings of Our Lord, both the Church itself and Peter and his successors were to be divinely protected against making mistakes whenever they taught His doctrines. This is what is known as Papal Infallibility.

The Catholic Church has never failed to teach all the truths of Our Lord. The Catholic Church has never contradicted herself as the spiritual teacher of mankind. Never once has she taught anything contrary to the teachings of Christ. Only her possession of the great gift of infallibility can explain this.

Pope Pius IX believed the time had come to announce this Catholic truth of Papal Infallibility to the whole world. It was not something new. It was something very old. Only the formal statement of it by Pope and Bishops united at the Vatican Council was new.

The decision was approved and applauded by the vast majority of those present. A few thought that the solemn pronouncement of this doctrine should be postponed until a later time. These however gave their approval as soon as the doctrine of Papal Infallibility was announced.

The spiritual glory of the Vatican Council made up for the temporal loss of the Papal States.

War with Bismarck

UP TO the nineteenth century Germany was a small country in the control of Austria. Otto von Bismarck made Germany an Empire. In 1866 the troops of Germany defeated Austria in a seven weeks war. In 1870 Germany defeated France.

In the same year the Vatican Council declared that the Pope was infallible in so far as matters of faith and morals is concerned.

A few Catholic teachers in Germany refused to accept the decision of the Vatican Council. The Church in Germany ordered them to give up their positions as teachers in Catholic schools. Bismarck hastened to their defense. Bismarck was not interested in whether Catholics accepted the infallibility of the Pope or not. He was interested in destroying the Church. The loyalty of German Catholics to the Church angered him.

Priests who tried to defend their Church were arrested. Catholic schools were closed. The Jesuits, the Vincentians, the Redemptorists, the Fathers of the Holy Ghost and the Sisters of the Sacred Heart were banished from the Empire.

Protestants were placed in charge of all Catholic affairs in Germany. By the May Laws of 1873 all priests and Bishops were made employees of the state. Catholic seminaries were placed in the control of the government.

Wise as he was in the ways of the world Bismarck was not so wise in the ways of God. Bishops and priests and people in Germany stood solidly together. In the German parliament great Catholic leaders like Windhorst and Reichensperger and Mallinckrodt, who had always been loyal to their country, announced that they would remain loyal also to their God. The elections of 1877 increased the members of the Catholic or Center Party in the German Parliament. Sincere Protestants joined with Catholics against the tyranny of Bismarck.

The "Iron Chancellor," as Bismarck was called, had to surrender. Against the power of God and His Church the "Iron Chancellor" had feet of clay.

One by one the laws against Catholic Bishops and priests and schools and religious orders were removed. The church did not need Bismarck, but Bismarck needed the Church to defend his country against the Socialists.

Once again a modern Caesar had tried to destroy the Church in vain.

Apostle of Health

THE name of Louis Pasteur is the name of one of the greatest scientists in the history of the world. It was Louis Pasteur who first vaccinated people to save them from disease, and who showed the way to conquer harmful bacteria.

He was born in France in 1822. He died in 1895. Throughout his long life he devoted himself to science. We now know that the causes of most diseases are little living organisms or germs, called bacteria. They cannot be seen by the naked eye. Sometimes we breathe them into our lungs. They are present in much of the food which we eat. It is necessary to eat properly and to sleep well if we wish to resist them.

It was Louis Pasteur who studied these germs and who discovered the way to overcome them. He found them everywhere. A certain germ had destroyed the entire silk industry of France. Louis Pasteur was able to destroy this germ. He cured the whole world from the disease known as rabies, which generally follows the bite of a mad dog or other mad animal. He made safe for our use the world's milk and water supply.

All of these germs or bacteria are not harmful to man. Certain of them cause fermentation. As a result the juice of grapes is turned into wine.

Although he discovered this, Louis Pasteur refused to take charge of the wine industry of France. He preferred to devote his life to the saving of human lives.

He loved science. He also loved his religion. He saw the hand of God in everything. He could not understand how any scientist could deny God. The wonders of science are the wonders of God. They are not the wonders of man.

All his life he remained a good Catholic. The people of the province of Brittany in France are called Bretons. They are devout Catholics. Louis Pasteur wrote the following message to his children.

"The more I know, the more nearly is my faith that of the Breton peasant. Could I but know all I would have the faith of a Breton peasant woman."

Louis Pasteur defended the world against disease. He also defended the Church against the world. He was a true scientist and a true Catholic.

Miracle of Lourdes

ONE day a little girl of fourteen years of age was passing by a rocky cave near her native town. She was seeking wood for the winter fire for her parents were very poor. She was all alone, as her companions had gone on ahead of her.

Suddenly she heard the sound of wind. She looked toward the nearby trees, but they were not shaking. She looked again. This time in the niche of a rocky grotto she saw the figure of a lady. The lady was clothed in a white garment with a blue sash. There were golden roses at her feet. Her face was sweet and full of smiles. A rosary was in her hand.

The day was February 11, 1858. The little girl was Saint Bernadette Soubirous. The rock was the Grotto of Lourdes. The lady was the Blessed Virgin. This apparition or vision was the first of eighteen which Our Blessed Mother granted to Bernadette. The last apparition took place on July 16, 1858, the feast of Our Lady of Mount Carmel.

Many were the messages which Our Lady gave to Bernadette. She told Bernadette to drink the water from a spring which suddenly appeared at the foot of the Grotto. She bade Bernadette have the priests erect a Church on the spot. And then, in one of the apparitions, Our Blessed Lady revealed who she was: "I am the Immaculate Conception."

The Bishop of the diocese appointed a committee to study the apparitions. After a few years the apparitions were proven to be true. A church was erected on the spot.

Saint Bernadette joined the Sisters of Charity at Nevers, France. She never returned to Lourdes. She remained sweet and humble and holy all her life. In 1879 she died. In 1935 Pope Pius XI declared her a Saint.

Over six hundred thousand pilgrims go every year to Lourdes, where hundreds of cures have been made. Each miraculous cure has been investigated by a group of non-Catholic as well as Catholic doctors.

The shrine of Our Lady of Lourdes is known throughout the world. Hundreds of thousands have returned to God because one day Mary, the Immaculate Conception, appeared to a little peasant girl in a lonely cavern near the Pyrenees in Southern France.

91

Pope of the Workingman

ON MAY 15, 1891, one of the most important letters in the world was written. This letter was written in Latin by Pope Leo XIII. He was born in 1810. He became Pope in 1878. He died in 1903.

This letter was addressed by the Pope to the whole world. It is therefore known as an "Encyclical Letter." The first two Latin words of this letter are *"Rerum Novarum."* It is also known in English as the Encyclical Letter on the "Condition of Labor."

All during his long life Pope Leo XIII was interested in working people. Once, before he was Pope, in the city of Perugia, in Italy, he founded a savings bank for the benefit of workingmen.

The Catholic Church has always been the friend of the workingmen and the poor. Sometimes we refer to all working people as the "masses." The word "mass" refers to the Holy Sacrifice which is celebrated at the altar of every Catholic Church every morning. The Catholic Church has been called the "Church of the Mass and the Church of the masses."

In the very beginning of her history the Catholic Church demanded that the Roman Empire do away with slavery. Every man and woman, she taught, is precious and equal in the sight of God. Every man and woman has a right to work and to receive just wages for this work.

This is what is known as Social Justice. The Catholic Church has always fought for Social Justice.

In the nineteenth century wicked and selfish men, who called themselves "Liberals," refused to give men and women a living wage. They even allowed little children to work in factories for long hours and for little pay. They refused to permit workingmen to unite in unions.

No one dared raise a voice against them, that is, no one except Pope Leo XIII. He was not afraid of them.

Therefore he wrote his famous *"Labor Encyclical."* In it he demanded that workers be allowed to form unions, that they be paid a living wage, and that the employment of women and children for long hours in factories be forbidden.

No wonder Leo XIII is called the Pope of the Workingman, and is revered by the masses who toil by the sweat of their brows!

Pope of the Eucharist

UPON the election of Pope Pius X (1903-1914), a great and saintly parish priest became the Vicar of Our Lord and Savior Jesus Christ upon this earth. At the time of his election Pope Pius X was Archbishop of Venice. He chose as his motto the obligation "To Restore all Things in Christ."

The modern world was drifting back to paganism. Modern pagans worshiped no God except themselves. They lived for pleasure and for power. Once again it became necessary for the Church to point out the evils of the world.

In 1907 this simple Pope of the poor drew up a list of all the wicked errors that were deceiving men, and condemned them. In 1905 Pope Pius X urged the frequent and daily reception of the Holy Eucharist. Little children were to be permitted to receive Holy Communion as soon as they reached the age of reason.

Frequent reception of the Holy Eucharist brings Our Lord more closely to ourselves. Through Holy Communion every Catholic becomes a stronger soldier in the Church.

Pope Pius X heard that foreign rubber merchants were oppressing the Indians in Peru. He denounced the merchants for their greed and cruelty in their treatment of the Red men.

His heart was also saddened by the attitude of the French government towards the Church. By the wicked "Associations Law" all religious communities in France were exiled. In 1902 three thousand religious schools were closed. In 1906 France became an enemy of the Church.

Pope Pius X arranged to have all the laws of the Church clearly stated in a single volume. This is the new Code or book of Canon Law which was completed by Benedict XV.

The Pius X School of Liturgical Music founded in New York City in 1918 reminds us of the gentle Pope's love of sacred music.

When he died in the opening year of the World War he had prepared the Church for the great struggles that were to come. Together with Leo XIII, Benedict XV and Pius XI, Pope Pius X was one of the greatest among the spiritual and temporal leaders of the twentieth century.

The Catholic Church conquered the paganism of Ancient Rome. The Catholic Church will also conquer the paganism of our day.

Pope of Peace

IN 1914 the World War began. In the same year Pope Pius X died. He was succeeded by Pope Benedict XV.

Pope Benedict XV made every effort to stop the war. He exercised charity towards all victims of the war, no matter what their nationalities might be.

The word "Catholic" means universal. Because the Church is catholic, she has sons and daughters in every country throughout the world. Pope Benedict XV denounced the war but he remained strictly neutral. He denounced the invasion of Belgium by the Germans. He also denounced the starvation of the people of Germany and Austria by the Allies.

His heart bled especially for the innocent victims of the war. Collections were taken up in all Catholic churches for the relief of the people of Poland and Lithuania. For the starving children of Germany and Austria alone Pope Benedict collected the huge sum of three million dollars.

He demanded that all prisoners of war be treated with justice and charity. Pope Benedict XV denounced injustice everywhere, and exalted charity.

Even the League of Nations praised him for his fairness and for his charitableness.

In 1917 Benedict XV begged the nations to stop fighting. He begged them to reduce their armies and to submit their troubles to international arbitration. The rulers of the world ignored his appeal. Only President Wilson replied. Although the President did not try to end the war, he agreed with most of the Pope's plan for peace.

Unfortunately, for world peace, Pope Benedict XV was not invited to the Peace Conference at Versailles, at the close of the World War. The men who went to Versailles were not peacemakers. They were filled with hatred for their enemies.

The spirit of hatred dictated peace. The spirit of love was kept away. Had the Pope been present, the world might have been saved the terrible results which the Peace of Versailles has caused, because the treaty was written in hatred and in haste.

Worn out with his labors for all people in all countries Pope Benedict XV died in 1922. He had been faithful to the words of Our Lord:

"Blessed are the peacemakers for they shall be called the children of God."

COURAGE

PEACE

Apostle of Patriotism

IT IS the year 1914. At a desk in his residence in the Belgian city of Malines a tall and strong and aging man is seated. In his ears there is a rumble of war. The troops of Germany have crossed the borders. They already are on his country's soil, the sacred soil of Belgium. He straightens the episcopal ring upon his finger. He goes down the stairs and out into the street. Women kneel when they see him. Old men weep tears of joy. They are not to face the enemy alone. Their Archbishop is with them. Cardinal Mercier, Archbishop of Malines, scholar and patriot, is passing by.

Little he knew, when he was ordained a priest in 1874, that one day all Belgium would look upon him as its saviour. From 1882 to 1906, in obedience to the great Pope Leo XIII, he taught the philosophy of Saint Thomas Aquinas in the University of Louvain.

In 1906 the beloved teacher of Louvain was made a Cardinal and Archbishop of Malines. He became the greatest man in Belgium. Non-Catholics as well as Catholics united in honoring him. The Belgian Royal Academy demanded that he become their President.

And then suddenly, the horrors and bloodshed of war broke around him. He protested against the invasion of his country. He refused to leave. When the war ended, he had taken the highest place in the heart of Belgium as well as in the heart of the world.

So beloved had he become and so confident were men in his wisdom and learning that in 1924 certain members of the Anglican Church of England came to him and conversed with him about the possibility of bringing back the Anglican Church to the bosom of the Catholic Church.

These talks have become known as the "Malines Conversations." Nothing would have pleased the aging Cardinal more than the consummation of those ideas expressed at Malines.

The stream of his life, however, was nearing the eternal sea. In 1926 he died. All the famous men in Europe attended his funeral in the Church of Saint Gudule in Brussels.

His body lies in Malines. His soul is with God. His memory is in the heart of all patriots. Cardinal Mercier is the modern apostle of patriotism.

Wonder of Lisieux

THE most revered title in the Catholic Church is not the title of Pope or Cardinal or Archbishop or Bishop or Priest or Nun or Brother. The greatest title is that of "Saint."

The Church gives the title of "Saint" only to those who lead very holy lives and only after they have passed from the earthly scene of their many holy activities.

There are two great Saints known by the name of Teresa in the Catholic Church. One was a Spaniard, born in Old Castile. The other was a Frenchwoman, born in Alengon. Both were members of a religious order known as the Carmelites. One lived for sixty-seven years. The other lived for only twenty-four years. One was canonized, or declared a Saint, in 1622. The other was canonized in 1925.

These two Saints are Saint Teresa of Avila (1515-1582) and Saint Teresa of Lisieux (1873-1897). The latter is also known as the Little Flower of Jesus. She said that she would spend her heaven doing good upon earth. She also promised the people of Lisieux that she would let fall a shower of roses upon the earth after she died.

When only fifteen, Saint Teresa entered the Carmelite Convent in Lisieux. She realized that she was only a weak little girl. Yet, she asked Our Lord to use her life in any way He wished. She prayed particularly for the welfare of priests.

She was not asked by Our Lord to do great things like Saint Joan of Arc. She did little things well. She endured all her physical sufferings with patience and humility. Her life became the wonder of the little French town of Lisieux, where her religious habit, or clothes, may yet be seen. A magnificent church has been erected there by those who wished to show their love for her.

The whole world has fallen in love with her. Millions of Catholics and non-Catholics have honored her. She was unknown during her life. She became known to all the world only after her gentle spirit had passed from the earth.

To love God and to be loved by God is everything.

It is only the Saints who are truly great. May the Little Flower always pray for us and may the perfume of her holiness make our souls, like hers, a garden of love.

Pope Pius XI

O N FEBRUARY 6, 1922, Achille Ratti, Cardinal-Archbishop of the glorious city of Milan, succeeded Pope Benedict XV as the spiritual ruler of the Catholic Church. The new Pope chose the name of Pius XI.

As a priest young Father Achille Ratti had been ordained for the arch-diocese of Milan. His career as a student in Rome had been most brilliant. There he had mastered Catholic Philosophy, Catholic Theology and Canon Law. On his return to Milan he was appointed a teacher in the Milan seminary. In addition he was made chaplain to the Cenacle Convent.

There, after long hours of teaching and study, he preached to the Nuns of the Cenacle and instructed little children in the elements of our Holy Faith. Great in learning and humble in character, God destined him for great leadership.

Upon the death of a director of the Ambrosian Library, Father Achille Ratti succeeded to his post. He worked among the writings and manuscripts of scholars for twenty-two years, from 1888 to 1910. In 1910 Pope Benedict XV summoned him to Rome to take charge of the Vatican Library.

In 1918, at the close of the World War, Pope Benedict XV sent the future Pope to act as Papal Nuncio or representative to the city of Warsaw in Poland. Once again Poland had become an independent State among the family of nations of Europe, and one of the Church's most trusted servants was sent to celebrate her return.

At the end of three years, Archbishop Ratti was made Cardinal-Archbishop of his native diocese of Milan. He was less than a year in Milan when Pope Benedict XV died. Cardinal Achille Ratti became the new Pope.

No Pope has ever done more for the glory of God and for the service of humanity. Stirred by the sufferings of the poor and the working people, Pope Pius XI wrote his famous Encyclical Letter on "*The Reconstruction of the Social Order*," May 15, 1931.

He insisted that all workers be paid a living wage. He called on all classes of people to live and work in peace. He praised the Encyclical Letter on the Condition of Labor which Pope Leo XIII had written fifty years previous. Like Pope Leo XIII, Pope Pius XI stands out as the friend and defender of the poor.

VATICAN CITY

VATICAN CITY, or the Vatican State, is that part of the city of Rome which does not belong to Italy. It belongs to the Church. Its ruler is the Pope. It consists of only 160 acres of land. It is like a large park. Vatican City has only about three hundred inhabitants. They are subjects of the Pope and not subjects of the King of Italy. Vatican City has existed since February 11, 1929.

Since September 20, 1870, Pope Pius IX, Pope Leo XIII, Pope Pius X, Pope Benedict XV and Pope Pius XI remained prisoners in the Vatican. They remained there as a protest against the unjust seizure of the Papal States by the troops of Garibaldi and King Victor Emmanuel.

In the year 1929, however, both Pope Pius XI and Benito Mussolini, entered into discussions in order to settle this "Roman Question."

The Italian people, who are Catholics, were grieved to think that their Pope was not free and independent. Catholics throughout the world did not want their Pope to be the temporal subject of any earthly King or ruler. Benito Mussolini himself realized that the Church should possess some lands over which no temporal ruler had any power.

The Church did not ask for all the States that were taken away from her in 1870. She was glad that the Italian people were a united nation. Pope Pius XI desired the smallest possible bit of territory, as a symbol rather than as a temporal dominion. He did not desire to become a powerful earthly ruler. He knew that his rule was over the things that are of the spirit.

After long discussions the "Roman Question" was finally settled. Cardinal Gasparri represented the Pope. Benito Mussolini represented the King of Italy. By the Lateran Treaty of February 11, 1929, Italy renounced her rule over 160 acres situated in the city of Rome. Vatican City was turned over to the Church. At the same time a Concordat or agreement was signed between Vatican City and Italy. Each admitted the existence and rights of the other.

The voluntary imprisonment of the Vatican was over. A short time later Pope Pius XI left the Vatican and rode through Rome. He was the first Pope to leave the Vatican since the days of Pope Pius IX.

Catholicism vs. Communism

SINCE 1918 Communist leaders, such as Lenin and Stalin, have oppressed the Russian people. Russia has been turned into a large prison camp.

All citizens in the United States possess freedom of speech, freedom of the press, freedom of assemblage, freedom of education and freedom of religion. No Russian citizen possesses a single one of these rights.

The Russian tyrant Stalin has destroyed everyone who disagrees with him. No Russian newspaper dares utter a word against Stalin or the Russian government. No one but a Communist can be elected to the Russian government.

Workers in the United States have the right to go on strike.

No Russian worker is allowed to strike. Many Russian peasants are forced to wear shoes of straw. The average Russian worker is paid a starvation wage. Russian women are forced to work in Russian mines and factories. Russian women are also obliged to join the army in order to fight in some future war. No Russian man or woman would dare protest against these terrible conditions. If they did, they would lose their lives.

Communism in Russia is the enemy of God as well as the enemy of the Russian people. The Bible may not be printed in the Russian language. Churches have been destroyed. Priests and bishops have been murdered. All religious activities are prohibited. The Communist government of Russia encourages all people to join a society called the "Union of Militant Atheists."

The Catholic Church has always been the enemy of paganism. She opposes paganism in Germany as well as in Russia. The Catholic Church stands opposed to any government which deprives the people of their rights.

One of the Communist leaders in America boasts that Communism wants to root out the notion of God and the supernatural from the minds of men. All Protestants and Jews and Catholics must unite against it.

In his Encyclical letter on *"Atheistic Communism"* March 19, 1937, Pope Pius XI offered the support of the Catholic Church in this battle against Communistic paganism and Communistic tyranny.

Communism is the greatest enemy of the United States of America today. No Catholic and no real American can have anything to do with Communism.

The Church Marches On

AS WE look backwards across the nineteen centuries which have passed since the Birth of Our Lord, we should be proud that we are Catholics. The Ages of Faith were ages of great happiness.

There is nothing to apologize for in the long history of the Catholic Church. We have to apologize only for those who deserted the Church. We do not condemn a family because one of its members has been disloyal to the laws of God and man. The Catholic Church is a large family whose head is Christ. That is what we mean by the Mystical Body of Christ.

We must be on our guard against certain histories that are written about the Catholic Church. Enemies of the Catholic Church are not fair when they write about her two thousand years of ministry. They allow their personal feelings to carry them away from the truth.

When anyone makes a charge against the Catholic Church we should insist that his charge be proven. We should insist that the critic read Catholic history from Catholic sources as well as from non-Catholic sources.

Whatever can be criticised in the history of the Catholic Church is purely human. No criticism can be made of her Founder, Our Lord and Savior Jesus Christ. No criticism can be made of her Saints. No criticism can be made of her doctrines or morality or Sacraments.

It was the Catholic Church that brought the message of Christ to men. It was the Catholic Church which civilized the world. For that she deserves the gratitude of the world of today.

Any institution has a right to be judged on the basis of her best or on the basis of her average and never on the basis of her worst. We praise the Colonial Army for the career of George Washington. We do not blame the Colonial Army for the career of a Benedict Arnold. We should demand the same fairness from those who write about the history of the Catholic Church.

The wealth of the Catholic Church consists of four items which we should never forget:

1. Buildings erected for the glory of Almighty God.
2. Buildings erected for the service of humanity. These are our Catholic schools, hospitals, libraries, museums, orphanages, homes for the aged, universities, day nurseries etc.

3. The great religious communities and orders whose members take voluntary vows of poverty, chastity and obedience in order to devote their lives to God and to men.

Our greatest wealth is our greatest poverty. Without these voluntary vows of poverty taken by religious men, called priests and brothers, and by religious women, called nuns, the Catholic Church could not have educated or civilized the world or maintained her charities, which stretch like a rosary around the earth.

4. The voluntary donations and sacrifices of all individual Catholics.

Catholic men and women are also the wealth of the Church. In the United States, for instance, Catholic men and women have built the Church and supported her program of education and charity, through the offerings they willingly make every Sunday.

These four items constitute the wealth of the Church. When anyone attacks the wealth of the Church they are attacking all Catholics. For true Catholics are the real wealth of the Catholic Church.

The Catholic Church today is still persecuted in many countries. She is free in the United States of America. She will remain free in America, and she will regain her freedom elsewhere, if we Catholics will only remain true to her.

By remaining true to the Catholic Church we are remaining true to our government. For as Catholics we are taught to obey all legitimate governments.

By remaining true to the Catholic Church we shall contribute to the civilization of the world because the Catholic Church has been the mother of civilization.

By remaining true to the Catholic Church we shall remain true to Our Lord and Savior Jesus Christ. It was Our Lord who died for us. It was Our Lord who founded the Catholic Church. It was Our Lord who said of the Catholic Church:

"He that heareth you, heareth me."

Quiz Review

O N THE following pages the reader will find five hundred questions based upon the text of the hundred *Great Moments in Catholic History*. Where the book is used as a textbook in Catholic schools the questions will serve as a convenient review test of the information gained in the corresponding chapters in the text. Where the book is used as a ready reference in the Catholic home, the popular "quiz" form of the questions will supply both entertainment and enlightenment to every member of the family. To be able to answer all of these five hundred questions correctly means that you have gained a true knowledge of the Catholic Church, as she was founded, as she progressed through twenty centuries, and as she stands in all her glory today.

1. *What day is the feast of the Annunciation?*
2. *What do you mean by the Annunciation?*
3. *Where do we read about the Annunciation?*
4. *Who is the greatest woman in the history of the world?*
5. *Name two prayers which recall the Annunciation.*

(Answers will be found on page 1)

* * *

1. *What does the word Bethlehem mean?*
2. *Why did Mary and Joseph travel from Nazareth to Bethlehem?*
3. *What treatment did they receive in the city?*
4. *Where was Our Lord born?*
5. *What did the angels sing on the night that Christ was born?*

(Answers will be found on page 2)

* * *

1. *How old was Our Lord when He began His public life?*
2. *What do you mean by the Jewish feast of the Passover?*
3. *Name three things which Our Lord did at the Last Supper.*
4. *What is meant by the Mass?*
5. *What is meant by Holy Communion?*

(Answers will be found on page 3)

* * *

1. *What is Good Friday?*
2. *Why did Our Lord die?*
3. *What accusation was made against Our Lord before the court of Caiphas?*
4. *What accusation was made against Our Lord before the court of Pontius Pilate?*
5. *Whom did the Jews choose to free instead of Our Lord?*

(Answers will be found on page 4)

* * *

1. *Name three important gardens in the history of the world.*
2. *Who asked Pilate for the body of Our Lord?*
3. *Who went to anoint the body of Our Lord in the tomb?*
4. *To whom did Our Lord reveal Himself in the Easter garden?*
5. *Why is Easter the greatest feast in the calendar of the Church?*

(Answers will be found on page 5)

* * *

1. *How many days after Easter did Our Lord ascend into heaven?*
2. *What did Our Lord say to the Apostles before He went?*
3. *In what book of the Bible do we read about the Ascension?*
4. *What was the first form of Catholic Action?*
5. *In what Church do we still find Our Lord?*

(Answers will be found on page 6)

* * *

1. *What do you mean by Pentecost?*
2. *When is the feast of Pentecost celebrated?*
3. *What change took place in the Apostles?*
4. *How many converts did St. Peter make by his first sermon?*
5. *Why is Pentecost called the birthday of the Catholic Church?*

(Answers will be found on page 7)

* * *

1. *Whom did Our Lord make the first Pope?*
2. *By what name did Our Lord call him?*
3. *What was his original name?*
4. *In what city did he die?*
5. *Who was the brother of the first Pope?*

(Answers will be found on page 8)

* * *

1. *Who was the first martyr in the Catholic Church?*
2. *What were the duties of the first deacons?*
3. *What do you mean by the Acts of the Apostles?*
4. *What is the meaning of the word martyr?*
5. *Quote what the first martyr said just before he died.*

(Answers will be found on page 9)

* * *

1. *Where was Saint Paul born?*
2. *To what race did he belong*
3. *What was his other name?*
4. *Why did Saint Paul travel from Jerusalem to Damascus?*
5. *Who appeared to him on the journey?*

(Answers will be found on page 10)

* * *

1. Where were the followers of Our Lord first called Christians?
2. Give the dates of Saint Paul's first missionary journey.
3. Give the dates of Saint Paul's second missionary journey.
4. Give the dates of Saint Paul's third missionary journey.
5. Why is Saint Paul called the Apostle of the Gentiles?

(Answers will be found on page 11)

* * *

1. What do you mean by the last gospel of the Mass?
2. Who wrote it?
3. Why is this Apostle called the divine?
4. Why is this Apostle called the beloved?
5. What is the name of the last book of the Bible?

(Answers will be found on page 12)

* * *

1. What do you mean by a Church Council?
2. What was the name of the first Catholic Council?
3. Where do we read about it?
4. To what race did the first converts belong?
5. Why was this Council called?

(Answers will be found on page 13)

* * *

1. Why did Catholics refuse to worship the Roman Emperor as god?
2. How did the Roman Emperors punish them?
3. What was the Coliseum?
4. For how many years was the Church persecuted in the very beginning
5. Name some of the Emperors who persecuted her?

(Answers will be found on page 14)

* * *

1. How deep were the Catacombs?
2. What were the Catacombs used for?
3. Why did the early Christians have to use the Catacombs?
4. When did the early Christians stop building Catacombs?
5. What do the Catacombs teach us about the early Church?

(Answers will be found on page 15)

* * *

1. Who were Constantine's father and mother?
2. How did he become Emperor?
3. Who was his opponent?
4. What happened at the Milvian Bridge?
5. Who received Constantine into the Church?

(Answers will be found on page 16)

* * *

1. Why did the Roman persecutions fail to destroy our religion?
2. Which Roman Emperor asked the Christians to pray for him?
3. Which Roman Emperor gave freedom to the Church?
4. What is the name of this document which gave freedom to the Church?
5. Why is the blood of martyrs called the seed of the Church?

(Answers will be found on page 17)

* * *

1. At what part of the Mass does the priest recite the Nicene Creed?
2. Why is it called the Nicene Creed?
3. What false doctrine was taught by Arius?
4. What is a heretic?
5. What is the name of the Saint who opposed the heretic Arius?

(Answers will be found on page 18)

* * *

1. What do you mean by the True Cross?
2. Who discovered it?
3. When and where was it discovered?
4. Why is it wrong to say that Catholics worship relics?
5. Name the two days on which we celebrate the Finding and Exaltation of the True Cross.

(Answers will be found on page 19)

* * *

1. What do you mean by an apostate?
2. What Roman Emperor became an apostate?
3. In what century did he live?
4. Of what city was Saint Ambrose Bishop?
5. Why did Saint Ambrose reprove the Emperor Theodosius?

(Answers will be found on page 20)

* * *

1. Who was the mother of Saint Augustine?
2. Where and when was Saint Augustine born?
3. Did Saint Augustine follow the teaching of his mother?
4. Which great Saint converted him?
5. Name two books which Saint Augustine wrote after he became a Catholic.

(Answers will be found on page 21)

* * *

1. During what years did Saint Jerome live?
2. Which Pope was his friend?
3. What language did all people speak at this time?
4. What is the Bible?
5. Why is Saint Jerome's translation called the Vulgate?

(Answers will be found on page 22)

* * *

1. Why was Attila called The Scourge of God?
2. Who were the Huns?
3. What Roman general saved France from the Huns?
4. How did the modem city of Venice start?
5. Which Pope saved Rome?

(Answers will be found on page 23)

* * *

1. Around what sea did the Roman Empire extend?
2. What people lived in northern Europe at the time of the Roman Empire?
3. Were these people civilized?
4. Why did the Roman Empire become weak?
5. In what year was the last Roman Emperor in the west killed?

(Answers will be found on page 24)

* * *

1. When was Saint Benedict born?
2. When did he begin to devote his life to God?
3. What three vows do members of religious orders take?
4. What useful works did the Benedictine monks do?
5. How many Saints did the Benedictine order produce?

(Answers will be found on page 25)

* * *

1. Which Pope brought about the conversion of England?
2. What did he call the English boys whom he saw in Rome?

3. Who was sent by the Pope to convert England?
4. In what century were the English converted?
5. Who was King of England at that time?

(Answers will be found on page 26)

* * *

1. Who were the Lombards?
2. Who is called Servant of the Servants of God?
3. To what religious order did Pope Gregory the Great belong.
4. What is the Breviary?
5. What did the Dialogues of Pope Gregory the Great contain?

(Answers will be found on page 27)

* * *

1. How did Saint Patrick first come to Ireland?
2. When did he return?
3. How long did he work among the Irish?
4. Who later tried to destroy the work of St. Patrick!
5. Did they succeed?

(Answers will be found on page 28)

* * *

1. Who were the Franks?
2. What modern country used to be called Gaul?
3. Who was the wife of King Clovis?
4. How did Clovis become a Catholic?
5. When was Clovis King of the Franks?

(Answers will be found on page 29)

* * *

1. What was Ireland called in the seventh century?
2. Who founded the great Scottish Abbey of Iona⁷
3. What Irish Saints preached in Switzerland⁷.
4. Who was Saint Boniface?
5. What was his original name?.

(Answers will be found on page 30)

* * *

1. What is meant by the Patrimony of Saint Peter?
2. Which Frankish Kings gave lands to the Pope?
3. Name a famous Catholic woman who left her possessions to the Church.
4. In what part of Italy were the Papal States?
5. Of what use to the Church were the lands she possessed?

(Answers will be found on page 31)

* * *

1. What do you mean by Mohammedanism?
2. What is meant by the Hegira?
3. What is the Koran?
4. Was Mohammedanism a religion of peace?
5. For how many years did Mohammedanism threaten to destroy Christianity?

(Answers will be found on page 32)

* * *

1. Which Catholic hero saved Europe from the followers of Mohammed?
2. In what year did the followers of Mohammed cross into France?
3. Why was it necessary to stop them?
4. At what city were they defeated?
5. What was the result of the battle?

(Answers will be found on page 33)

* * *

1. Why do we have pictures and images of Our Lord and Saints in our Churches?
2. What does the word Iconoclasm mean?
3. Which ruler of Constantinople wished to destroy all images?
4. Which Pope rebuked him?
5. Why is it wrong to say that Catholics worship images?

(Answers will be found on page 34)

* * *

1. Why did Charlemagne go to Rome?
2. Which Pope was his friend?
3. Was Charlemagne merely a soldier?
4. On what day and in what year was he crowned Emperor?
5. Why did the Pope crown him Emperor?

(Answers will be found on page 35)

* * *

1. Who were the two great Apostles of the Slavs?
2. In what century did they live?
3. What language did they use in their preaching?
4. Which Saint invented the Slavonic alphabet?
5. Did Pope Adrian II approve their use of the Slavonic language?

(Answers will be found on page 36)

* * *

1. From what three modern countries did the Northmen come?
2. Why are they called Vikings?
3. Of what country did Canute the Great become King?
4. Who were the first missionaries to the Northmen?
5. Who was Saint Ansgar?

(Answers will be found on page 37)

* * *

1. Name a famous Roman Saint who freed slaves.
2. What do you mean by the word serf?
3. What work did the religious community of the Trinitarians do?
4. What do you mean by the Order of Our Lady of Ransom?
5. Why is the Catholic Church called the mother of freedom?

(Answers will be found on page 38)

* * *

1. What gift did Our Lord promise the Disciples before He died?
2. What was the Peace of God?
3. What was the Truce of God?
4. Who is the Prince of Peace?
5. Since what century have the most horrible wars been waged?

(Answers will be found on page 39)

* * *

1. What are the marks of a gentleman?
2. What did Our Lord say about meekness and mercy?
3. What do you mean by chivalry?
4. What were the duties of a knight?
5. What alone can make the world happy?

(Answers will be found on page 40)

* * *

1. What do you mean by the word guild?
2. What were the Merchant Guilds?
3. What were the Craft Guilds?
4. What do you mean by the word apprentice?
5. What did the poet Lowell say about life in the Middle Ages?

(Answers will be found on page 41)

* * *

1. Where is Palestine?
2. Who was governor of Judea in the time of Our Lord?
3. From what Latin word does the English word crusade come?
4. When did the First Crusade begin?
5. How many Crusades were there in all?

(Answers will be found on page 42)

* * *

1. What do you mean by the Holy Roman Empire?
2. What do you mean by the Investiture quarrel?
3. What name did Hildebrand select when he became Pope?
4. What German Emperor tried to interfere with the Church?
5. What happened at Canossa?

(Answers will be found on page 43)

* * *

1. What was the original name of Constantinople?
2. Why was it called Constantinople?
3. Which Patriarch refused to obey the Pope?
4. What do you mean by the word schism?
5. What do you mean by the word uniat?

(Answers will be found on page 44)

* * *

1. In what century did Saint Thomas à Becket live?
2. Who was King of England in the time of Saint Thomas à Becket?
3. How did this King try to interfere with the Church?
4. What position did Saint Thomas à Becket hold?
5. Who brought about the murder of Saint Thomas à Becket?

(Answers will be found on page 45)

* * *

1. When did the Turks recapture Jerusalem?
2. Who was their leader?
3. What is a mosque?
4. Who were the leaders of the Christian troops in the Third Crusade?
5. What was the result of this Third Crusade?

(Answers will be found on page 46)

* * *

1. In what century did Pope Innocent III live?
2. What French King was refused a divorce by Innocent III?
3. What kind of a King was King John of England?

4. What charter of liberties was secured by English Catholics?
5. In what year was this charter secured?

(Answers will be found on page 47)

* * *

1. What century is often called the greatest of centuries?
2. Who was the mother of Saint Louis of France?
3. What did Saint Louis of France learn from his mother?
4. Why did Saint Louis fight against the Turks?
5. Where and when did he die?

(Answers will be found on page 48)

* * *

1. What do you mean by the word "poverello"?
2. What did Saint Francis do for the churches around Assisi?
3. In what year was the Franciscan Order established?
4. Who are the poor Clares?
5. What are the Stigmata of Saint Francis?

(Answers will be found on page 49)

* * *

1. What is meant by a religious community?
2. What is another name for them?
3. Who were the Albigenses?
4. When did Saint Dominic found the Dominicans?
5. What special devotion and prayer was used by Saint Dominic?

(Answers will be found on page 50)

* * *

1. Who was Saint Albert the Great?
2. What hymn did Saint Thomas write in honor of the Blessed Sacrament?
3. Why is Saint Thomas called the Angel of the Schools?
4. What is the name of Saint Thomas' greatest book?
5. What is meant by theology?

(Answers will be found on page 51)

* * *

1. What is meant by the saying that the school follows the Cross?
2. Name the oldest university in America.

3. Name some famous Catholic universities in Europe.
4. Who gave the Catholic Church the right and power to teach?
5. Why should Catholic boys and girls go to Catholic schools?

(Answers will be found on page 52)

* * *

1. What is meant by the word Gothic?
2. What are gargoyles?
3. Why were the first cathedrals of the Church called Romanesque?
4. What kind of arches were in Romanesque Cathedrals and in Gothic Cathedrals?
5. In what century did the Gothic Cathedrals become famous?

(Answers will be found on page 53)

* * *

1. Which Pope did most for Church music?
2. Who was Franz Haydn?
3. Name one hymn written by Cesar Franck.
4. Name one sacred song written by Franz Schubert.
5. Make a list of other famous Catholic musicians.

(Answers will be found on page 54)

* * *

1. What is meant by the word Renaissance?
2. In what century did the greatest Catholic artists live?
3. Name one work of Michelangelo.
4. Name one work of Raphael.
5. Name one work of Leonardo da Vinci.

(Answers will be found on page 55)

* * *

1. In what language were the books of the New Testament written?
2. Name one famous English Catholic who was an author.
3. Name one famous Italian Catholic who was an author.
4. Name one famous Spanish Catholic who was an author.
5. Name one famous French Catholic who was an author.

(Answers will be found on page 56)

* * *

1. Where is Avignon?
2. What do you mean by the Babylonian Captivity of the Church?

3. Which French King interfered with the freedom of the Church?
4. Which Pope opposed him?
5. Which Pope first became a prisoner at Avignon?

(Answers will be found on page 57)

* * *

1. Who was the savior of France in the fifteenth century?
2. Which King of France did she aid?
3. Where and in what year was she born?
4. What Saints appeared to her?
5. How did she die?

(Answers will be found on page 58)

* * *

1. What do you mean by the word manuscript?
2. Who preserved all ancient writings?
3. In what century was printing invented?
4. Who invented it?
5. Which book was printed first of all?

(Answers will be found on page 59)

* * *

1. What do you mean by the word Basilica?
2. What do you mean by the word Apse?
3. What do you mean by the word Narthex?
4. Name the four important basilicas in Rome.
5. In what centuries was the Vatican Basilica rebuilt?

(Answers will be found on page 60)

* * *

1. From what two tribes did the modem Spanish nation spring?
2. Who were the Moors?
3. When did they cross into Spain?
4. How long did they try to destroy the civilization of Spain?
5. Who drove them out of Spain?

(Answers will be found on page 61)

* * *

1. Name the ships of Columbus.
2. What Spanish queen helped him to make his voyages?
3. On what island did Christopher Columbus land?
4. How many voyages did Columbus make to America?
5. Where was Mass first said in the new world?

(Answers will be-found on page 62)

* * *

1. Name some of the Catholic explorers during the sixteenth century.

2. What part of the United States was civilized by the Spanish?
3. What part of the United States was civilized by the French?
4. How did the new world get the name America?
5. To what famous priest has a statue been erected in Washington?

(Answers will be found on page 63)

* * *

1. Who accompanied all the Spanish explorers?
2. What do you mean by the reductions in Paraguay?
3. What were the Indians taught?
4. What famous Dominican bishop protected the Indians in Mexico?
5. When was slavery abolished in Mexico?

(Answers will be found on page 64)

* * *

1. Does the Church wish all men to be holy?
2. Is she to blame for those who refuse to be holy?
3. Name three men who attempted to destroy the Church in the sixteenth century.
4. Which wicked leader admitted that the Protestant Reformation was a failure?
5. What was the purpose of the Council of Trent?

(Answers will be found on page 65)

* * *

1. How did Saint Ignatius of Loyola begin to serve Our Lord?
2. When was the Society of Jesus formed?
3. By what other name are the followers of Saint Ignatius of Loyola known?
4. To what great work did they devote themselves?
5. Who was the most famous of his companions?

(Answers will be found on page 66)

* * *

1. In what century did Saint Charles Borromeo live?
2. Of what city was he archbishop?
3. Which Pope was his uncle?
4. What did Saint Charles do in the midst of the plague?

5. How old was he when he died?

(Answers will be found on page 67)

* * *

1. Who were the Turks?
2. In what year did the Turks capture the city of Constantinople?
3. Where is the gulf of Lepanto?
4. Who was the leader of the Christian fleet?
5. In what year was the Turkish fleet destroyed at Lepanto?

(Answers will be found on page 68)

* * *

1. What do you mean by the Julian Calendar?
2. What do you mean by the Gregorian Calendar?
3. In what year did our modern calendar begin?
4. On what day did it begin?
5. Why did some countries refuse to adopt the Gregorian Calendar?

(Answers will be found on page 69)

* * *

1. Why was Henry VIII first called Defender of the Faith?
2. Who was his lawful wife?
3. What do you mean by the Act of Supremacy?
4. Which two Saints refused to accept it?
5. What did the monasteries suffer from Henry VIII?

(Answers will be found on page 70)

* * *

1. What religion did Edward VI bring into England?
2. To what religion did Queen Mary belong?
3. What promise did Queen Elizabeth make to Queen Mary?
4. Did Queen Elizabeth keep that promise?
5. Why do we call Queen Elizabeth the most bigoted and brutal of all English Queens?

(Answers will be found on page 71)

* * *

1. Who is Frederick Ozanam?
2. Who is St. Louise de Marrilac?
3. Who are the Vincentians?
4. Why are they called the Congregation of the Missions?
5. Among whom did Saint Vincent de Paul prefer to work?

(Answers will be found on page 72)

* * *

1. Name several of the Jesuit Martyrs in North America?
2. In what state did they preach to the Indians?
3. Why did the Iroquois Indians dislike them?
4. Who is the Lily of the Mohawks?
5. On what day do we celebrate their feast?

(Answers will be found on page 73)

* * *

1. Which three countries divided Poland among themselves?
2. When did this division take place?
3. When was Poland re-established as an independent nation?
4. In what century did the Polish King John Sobieski live?
5. What great work did he do for civilization?

(Answers will be found on page 74)

* * *

1. What is the source of all authority?
2. What is meant by inalienable rights?
3. Whose consent to govern must be possessed by a just government?
4. Name the two great Jesuit teachers of democracy.
5. In what American document did Thomas Jefferson use their teachings?

(Answers will be found on page 75)

* * *

1. Did the Pilgrim Fathers practice religious freedom in America?
2. What is the name of the priest who accompanied the Catholic settlers to Maryland?
3. In what year did Maryland pass an act of religious freedom?
4. Why did this act only mention Christians?
5. When was religious freedom first granted in New York?

(Answers will be found on page 76)

* * *

1. Name two Catholic signers of the Declaration of Independence.
2. To what religious order did Bishop Carroll belong?
3. Why did the Continental Congress send him to Canada?
4. In what year did Father Carroll become Bishop Carroll?

5. When and how did he become Archbishop of Baltimore?

(Answers will be found on page 77)

* * *

1. Were the California Missions merely Churches?
2. What were the Indians taught at the Missions?
3. What priest built the California Missions?
4. How many did he build?
5. What happened to the Indians when the Franciscan Friars left?

(Answers will be found on page 78)

* * *

1. Who is known as the Father of the American Navy?
2. Name some Catholic military geniuses from Europe who helped the colonists win the Revolution.
3. Which president thanked all Catholics for their loyalty in the Revolution?
4. Name some famous Catholic leaders in the World War.
5. What percent of the army, navy and marine corps were Catholic?

(Answers will be found on page 79)

* * *

1. Where was Napoleon born?
2. Why did he quarrel with Pope Pius VII?
3. What wrongs did he commit against the Pope?
4. During what years was Pius VII Pope?
5. Where and how did Napoleon die?

(Answers will be found on page 80)

* * *

1. How were Catholics persecuted in England and Ireland after Queen Elizabeth?
2. When did Catholics receive the right to vote?
3. When were Catholics in Ireland permitted to lease land?
4. What happened when Daniel O'Connell was first elected to Parliament?
5. In what year was the Catholic Emancipation Bill passed?

(Answers will be found on page 81)

* * *

1. To what religion did John Henry Newman first belong?
2. At what university did he teach?
3. In what year did Newman begin to write pamphlets?

4. What was the result of his studies in Church history?
5. In what year did he become a Cardinal?

(Answers will be found on page 82)

* * *

1. In what modern centuries was the Catholic Church persecuted?
2. In what countries was she persecuted?
3. Name one famous French Catholic of the nineteenth century.
4. Name one famous German Catholic of the nineteenth century.
5. What famous German Bishop was the friend of all workingmen?

(Answers will be found on page 83)

* * *

1. How many Catholics were in the United States at the close of the American Revolution?
2. In what states did they live?
3. How many Catholics are in the United States today?
4. In what years were the three Councils of Baltimore held?
5. What great work was established by the first Council of Baltimore?

(Answers will be found on page 84)

* * *

1. What famous Cathedral was begun by Archbishop Hughes?
2. When did he become Bishop of New York?
3. What particular work did Archbishop Hughes establish in New York?
4. Name two groups of people who tried to persecute Catholic citizens at this time.
5. Why did Archbishop Hughes go to France during the Civil War?

(Answers will be found on page 85)

* * *

1. Name three great English Cardinals in the nineteenth century.
2. Which ones among them were converts?
3. In what year did the Church appoint Bishops to England?
4. What happened in England when the Bishops returned?
5. Which Cardinal was noted for his love for the poor?

(Answers will be found on page 86)

* * *

1. Was Italy a united kingdom in the beginning of the nineteenth century?
2. Which Pope was asked to become the leader of the united Italy?
3. On what date was the city of Rome seized?
4. What do you mean by the Law of Guarantees?
5. Why did the Church refuse to accept this law?

(Answers will be found on page 87)

* * *

1. In what year was the Vatican Council held?
2. Why is it called the Vatican Council?
3. What do we mean when we say that the Pope is infallible?
4. What did Our Lord promise His Church?
5. Which Pope presided over the Vatican Council?

(Answers will be found on page 88)

* * *

1. In what century did Germany become an Empire?
2. How did Bismarck interfere with the Church?
3. What religious orders did he banish from the Empire?
4. Who was Windhorst?
5. Was Bismarck successful in his war against the Church?

(Answers will be found on page 89)

* * *

1. What are bacteria?
2. Are they all harmful?
3. Why is Louis Pasteur famous?
4. In what century did he live?
5. Besides being a great scientist, what other greatness did he possess?

(Answers will be found on page 90)

* * *

1. To whom did Our Lady appear at Lourdes?
2. On what day did she first appear?
3. How many times did she appear?
4. What did Our Lady call herself?
5. Why is Lourdes famous?

(Answers will be found on page 91)

* * *

1. *Give the Latin title of Pope Leo XIII's great letter?*
2. *Give its English title?*
3. *What is Social Justice?*
4. *What did Pope Leo XIII demand for the workingmen?*
5. *Of what wrongs against the workingmen were the Liberals of the nineteenth century guilty?*

(Answers will be found on page 92)

* * *

1. *During what years was Pius X Pope?*
2. *What motto did he choose?*
3. *What rules did Pope Pius X make about the reception of Holy Communion?*
4. *What country exiled nuns and priests in the time of Pope Pius X?*
5. *Name two other things for which Pope Pius X is famous.*

(Answers will be found on page 93)

* * *

1. *In what year did Benedict XV become Pope?*
2. *Why did the Pope have to remain neutral during the World War?*
3. *Why did the League of Nations praise Pope Benedict XV?*
4. *How did Pope Benedict XV try to stop the war?*
5. *Was Pope Benedict XV invited to the Peace Conference at Versailles?*

(Answers will be found on page 94)

* * *

1. *In what famous university did Cardinal Mercier teach?*
2. *Of what city did he become Archbishop?*
3. *What do you mean by the Malines Conversations?*
4. *Why do the people of Belgium love him?*
5. *When did he die?*

(Answers will be found on page 95)

* * *

1. *What is the greatest title that any Catholic can possess?*
2. *When did Saint Teresa of Avila live?*
3. *When did Saint Teresa of Lisieux live?*
4. *By what other name is Saint Teresa of Lisieux known?*
5. *How did she become holy?*

(Answers will be found on page 96)

* * *

1. *What is the family name of Pope Pius XI?*
2. *In what city did he first labor as a priest?*
3. *What work did he do there?*
4. *Where did Pope Benedict XV send him?*
5. *In what year did he himself become Pope?*

(Answers will be found on page 97)

* * *

1. *How large is Vatican City?*
2. *What is its population?*
3. *When did it begin to exist?*
4. *Why must the Pope be independent of all earthly rulers?*
5. *Which Pope settled the Roman Question?*

(Answers will be found on page 98)

* * *

1. *Name some liberties which we citizens of the United States possess.*
2. *Do Russian citizens possess them?*
3. *Are Russian workers allowed to strike?*
4. *How are Russian women forced to work?*
5. *Show that Communism is the enemy of God and of religion.*

(Answers will be found on page 99)

* * *

1. *What do you mean by the Mystical Body of Christ?*
2. *When anyone criticizes the Catholic Church what should we do?*
3. *On what basis should any institution be judged?*
4. *Name the four items which constitute the wealth of the Catholic Church.*
5. *Give three reasons why we should always remain true to the Catholic Church.*

(Answers will be found on page 100)

Hillside Education

www.hillsideeducation.com

EDITOR'S NOTE

Since this book was originally published in 1938, any great moments that have occurred since then are not included. There could certainly be many entries for the time of World War II and since the Second Vatican Council, moments with Pope Saint John XXIII and Pope Saint John Paul II. The Church continues to stand for human dignity and respect for life at every stage. Perhaps an activity you can do with your children is to research modern history to find those moments and make them into your own book.

There are several places where this book mentions the parts of the Mass; however, they refer to the Traditional or Extraordinary Mass. In the Ordinary Form, no longer does the priest read the first chapter of John's Gospel at the end of Mass, and the entire congregation recites the Creed during the Mass with the priest. We made the decision to not update the text, but leave it as Father Curran originally wrote it. If you attend the Ordinary Form, you can note these items to your child as they appear in the text. Also there is reference to Communist Russia at the end, and as you know, the situation with Russia has changed several times since Father Curran wrote this text. Once again, you will need to provide updated information about Russia for your children.

WANT TO LEARN MORE?

The following books published by Hillside Education are about events and people mentioned in this text. Check them out to learn more about Catholic History.

Charles Carroll and the American Revolution by Milton Lomask
> Mentioned on page 77: Catholic signer of the Declaration of Independence

Chuiraquimba and the Black Robes by Madeleine Polland
> Mentioned on page 64: the Jesuit missions in Paraguay

City of the Golden House by Madeleine Polland
> Mentioned on pages 8 and 11: martyrdom of St. Peter and St. Paul

Cross Among the Tomahawks by Milton Lomask
> Mentioned on page 73: the North American Martyrs

DeTonti of the Iron Hand by Ann Heagney
> Mentioned on page 63: explorations of LaSalle in North America

Fabiola by Cardinal Wiseman
> Mentioned on page 14: persecution of the early Church

Joan of Arc by Hilaire Belloc (Due out Spring 2017)
> Mentioned on page 58: the work of Joan of Arc

John Hughes, Eagle of the Church by Doran Hurley
> Mentioned on page 85: Archbishop of New York in nineteenth century

The Thrall of Leif the Lucky by Ottilie A Liljencrantz
> Mentioned on page 37: St. Olaf of Norway commissions Leif